Body Language

NLP Training to Become the Alpha Male
And Naturally Attract Women

*(Develop Communication Skills, Persuasion To
Influence People And Make real Success)*

Steven Pathway

Published By **Elena Holly**

Steven Pathway

All Rights Reserved

Body Language: NLP Training to Become the Alpha Male And Naturally Attract Women (Develop Communication Skills, Persuasion To Influence People And Make real Success)

ISBN 978-1-77485-795-3

No part of this guidebook shall be reproduced in any form without permission in writing from the publisher except in the case of brief quotations embodied in critical articles or reviews.

Legal & Disclaimer

The information contained in this ebook is not designed to replace or take the place of any form of medicine or professional medical advice. The information in this ebook has been provided for educational & entertainment purposes only.

The information contained in this book has been compiled from sources deemed reliable, and it is accurate to the best of the Author's knowledge; however, the Author cannot guarantee its accuracy and validity and cannot be held liable for any errors or omissions. Changes are periodically made to this book. You must consult your doctor or get professional medical advice before using any of the suggested remedies, techniques, or information in this book.

Upon using the information contained in this book, you agree to hold harmless the Author from and against any damages, costs, and expenses, including any legal fees potentially resulting from the application of any of the information provided by this guide. This disclaimer applies to any damages or injury caused by the use and application, whether directly or indirectly, of any advice or information presented, whether for breach of contract, tort, negligence, personal injury, criminal intent, or under any other cause of action.

You agree to accept all risks of using the information presented inside this book. You need to consult a professional medical practitioner in order to ensure you are both able and healthy enough to participate in this program.

Table of Contents

Chapter 1: Importance Body Language In Business World 1

Chapter 2: Manipulation In A Relationship..... 6

Chapter 3: Posture And Body Orientation ... 17

Chapter 4: 5 Surprising Truths Concerning Body Language.. 33

Chapter 5: Reading Body Movements 41

Chapter 6: Body Posture 57

Chapter 7: Head Action 73

Chapter 8: Body Language For Seduction 88

Chapter 9: Trust Your Intelligence..............103

Chapter 10: Different Physical Movements 113

Chapter 11: Popular Hand Gestures And Their Meanings In Different Cultures 131

Chapter 12: Body Language Of A Flirting Woman 134

Chapter 13: Common Patterns In Interpreting Behavior: Hands And Arms 139

Chapter 14: How To Spot A Lie - Key Behavior That Indicates Deception 146

Chapter 15: Charisma 154

Chapter 16: Tools To Say No 161

Conclusion 181

Chapter 1: Importance Body Language In Business World

Both in business communication and in personal communication, non-verbal communication has been shown significantly to impact our perception of others. You can frame your image communication and alter the business character by how you communicate with your partners, customers, and workers.

For business communication, these are the most important attributes that organizations can convey via non-verbal signs.

* Confidence. Throughout history, business visionaries as well as business pioneers have believed that they can trust the people and things they do. Take a look Richard Branson (Virgin Media). He exudes confidence and has a huge smile.

* assertiveness: It is an essential part of business communication. You must be confident, no matter what service you offer to customers.

* Interest: It is the best way to communicate when everyone is interested. Demonstrating enthusiasm for each conversation is a good sign of polished methodology. This is great for creating better customer and management brands.

* Intelligence. Body language techniques can even make it appear that people are more intelligent than they actually are. You can "conceal any hint" of failure in business communications by gesturing along, demonstrating cognizance and tutoring your face to not show perplexity when faced with ambiguous circumstances.

* Empathy. It is important to show empathy. If experts can respond to the passion needs of clients or partners, they

have the greatest chance to thrive in today's highly competitive marketplace.

There are many activities that you can do, and also many that you shouldn't do. Non-verbal communication is an important tool to increase your potential for success. No matter where you live, the first introductions are key to your success throughout your day. People can sometimes change their views when they size you up. Make sure to make the most of the first meeting.

Albert Mehrabian proved that body language was a significant and well-known way to judge the affability of someone. He found that non-verbal communication makes up 93% of communication. Languages only represent 7%. Dr. Albert Mehrabian looked at the various types of nonverbal communications. These included: appearances, pose, contact with, outward appearances and signals as well as manners of speaking and eye to eyes connection. It's not a good idea to ignore non-verbal communication's impact on your notoriety.

To create effective body language in business communications, you must understand how your coworkers are expected to present themselves during their daily conversations. Also, it is important to establish rules for nonverbal achievement. Some companies even offer nonverbal communication courses for their staff to make them more comfortable with this topic.

No matter where your situation is, it doesn't matter how good your communication skills may be. Truthfully, communication skills are a necessity with the goal of being effective in every area of one's life. Stay on top and make the right impression every time. You must be alert to your surroundings and others' activities in order to do this.

Pay attention to the non-verbal communication you use. This will allow you to be more creative. There are many things that you will be able to recall and you will quickly become proficient in them all. It doesn't take much to master body language. Do these three things and you won't be disappointed.

Listening to what's not said is the most important aspect of communication.

Chapter 2: Manipulation in A Relationship

Culture loves to romanticize deceptive relationships, even though it is difficult to recognize their true nature. Literature abounds with evidence that real relationships are about fixation. This suggests that pure love can transcend boundaries and have no separate lives.

People romanticize the idea that a deceptive partner is real love, even though it may seem like it. Sometimes, the romance may be dramatic and create tension. However, it is not fun to live in a deceptive romantic relationship.

Although manipulating people may be something you have been warned about, coercion or mistreatment are still worrying. The truth is that being in a controlled and manipulative relationship that never leads to ill-treatment can be scary and dangerous. However, just because someone doesn't physically hurt you, does not mean they aren't causing you pain.

Being dominated by or made to feel inferior by a partner can make us lose faith, cause us to be afraid for future relationships and leave us feeling helpless.

It is possible that you have experienced the negative effects of a relationship. You may have been in a relationship with a partner that required you to wear certain clothing items or prevented you from visiting your friends.

This person might ask you where you are and what you are up to. They may also want to know why you are late. Manipulators often have anxiety and let nervous thoughts pass through their brains to control their actions. We turn our fear and anxiety into hallucinations about how you will react if you're not around us. They will focus on their worst fears and the damage they can inflict upon you, and assume you are doing this when you are not there.

You may be hated by them if they do this. It may be flattering sometimes to have someone so concerned. You may think that it is nice for someone to be concerned about you. But, when they want to keep you safe, it is not their intent.

They do not care about your health. So the manipulators have this mindset: "I need my location to be able to tell them where they are at all times. This will ensure that they don't do any thing I don't like." Your presence can be used to reassure them that you aren't causing harm by doing the same thing as them. They won't address your concerns in this situation. The manipulator acts only in his own interest.

A manipulator won't say that, but will only want to make you feel better. They will continue to use this method to make sure that you feel guilty. They will make your feel guilty if it takes 20 minutes to reply, rather than admitting that it is normal for someone not to always respond immediately. They would consider you a traitor or dishonest because you didn't respond immediately or weren't available to answer their questions.

Marriage should feel better. It shouldn't be scary, confining, or distressing. Having a partner will make you more happy, not less. There will be some hard times in life. Your mate may not get you, or understand you. These difficulties should not be seen as obstacles. They can help you grow and become stronger. A healthy relationship should not drain you and tear you down, leaving you feeling constantly exhausted.

Signs you are in a manipulative partnership

Most people have suffered terrible things in life. For this reason, it can be tempting to look for a hero to sweep us off our feet. Sometimes, however, we find ourselves looking in the wrong place for safety, empathy, and care.

Check whether your partner might stop you from making the right decisions and living your best life. This partner is responsible for your maxed-out bank accounts. Talking to someone you have been struggling to talk to may not be a good idea.

True partners are aware that they cannot protect what is happening in your everyday life. Instead, they will support you as needed. If you have a money problem, a trusted friend can help. They will not give you your passwords. The best partner will not only offer their help, but will also be able to help you manage your problems.

One example of a manipulative relationship is when someone makes us feel guilty when we go to see our family and friends. Imagine someone trying to get rid of their partner and their emotionally supportive circle. In this scenario, the husband is threatening his wife with a TV drama in which he threatens her that she will never see her friend again. Deceptive spouses can still inconspicuously isolate one from the support network.

If you are cleverly manipulative, you won't discourage your family members from seeing you. In fact, it could be a sign you should be running in opposite direction. We will not force you to do something, but we will make it more subtle. Your manipulative partner can convince your partner to make you apologize for something that you have done correctly and admit that it is wrong.

Your partner can make a scene with your friends and then sulk until your partner is able to get rid of other friends. Maybe your partner will make negative comments towards your loved ones until it becomes clear that you are validating their views.

You might have a hobby you really enjoy and want your manipulator not to do it anymore. They will ridicule and make fun of you until your interest ceases.

However, it is not always easy to see the controlling partner's scrutiny. It's possible to make it reasonable and rational, meaning your partner might just be trying their best to help. They might even admit that they want to help.

They will investigate your decisions while you are at school. Their sentences might include the following: "Why are you choosing to use it in your presentation?" You don't care about what the boss thinks. They will be asking you questions about how you spend your money and what you buy. These manipulators will twist their words. It's not clear that the choices made are correct, but they will plant doubts and insecurity.

All partners need to be inspected by each other at least once a year. Still, our loved ones should look out for us. Sometimes we need to be aided by others to make the right choices or to point out bad habits. Make sure you always ask questions about the person and find out why they want you to change.

Sometimes manipulators may ask for access in an intimate relationship to your personal belongings, but they won't grant you those same rights. We may not be privy to all of your secrets but we do not trust you.

They are not only less likely to be social, but they are also not helping you.

This behavior is an indication that the partner controls. Your partner may not be able to access your texts and emails, nor ask for your passwords, unless they feel you are cheating. There is a fine line between having insider information and having healthy independence from your spouse. You don't have to give up that when you're in a relationship.

For couples to be able to heal from a crisis, it is necessary for the weaker spouses that they view each others' messages as a form transparent communication. This is not an agreement you reached directly with your spouse.

Coercion is the act of influencing someone else's thoughts and actions through emotional influence. Coercion may be disguised as emotion or even a kind of empathy. This is most often a deliberate effort of the manipulator to relate and comfort the victim.

To fully overcome manipulation, it is necessary to understand its effects on us. It is important to look at how our relationships have affected us in order to build a healthy and happy relationship. If it has a negative effect, it may be the first sign there is a manipulative partner.

People who manipulate others have four basic characteristics: they are able to recognize their weaknesses.

They use you vulnerabilities to their advantage.

They force you to share some of your personal resources to support their quick plots.

If a controller wins manipulating you, he is likely to repeat the crime until the mistreatment ceases.

They'll be able to control and keep you around for many reasons.

It may be because of a relationship that has ended. There may be confidence issues that have made them unable to communicate and think about other partners. This could make them feel as though they are trying to manipulate your loyalty.

Be aware of your rights in a relationship

It can be difficult when you are in an abusive relationship to figure out what to do.

Manipulators have a knack for creating uncertainty. The best way to keep yourself safe is to remind your rights.

These are the things you have the absolute right to take away, and should not be denied to another person. These principles will make manipulation easier to address as it happens. You'll also be better able to recognize when the conversation might be toxic.

However, these rights can be forfeited if you expose yourself to vulnerability. The following are your main human rights.

Expressions can be made of your thoughts, feelings, or emotions.

You retain the right to know your needs, to share them, and to do what is necessary to meet them, provided that you do not take away anything from others.

Chapter 3: Posture and Body Orientation

You can communicate a lot about yourself by how you sit and move when you interact. If this seems a little unclear, try this: Have any of you ever felt "suspicious" about someone who looks nice and talks nice? I don't mean that you have never felt that this person is trying to be superior, but despite his or her "nice" appearance. While you may not have known it, you actually picked up their body language, particularly their body positions, subconsciously. By looking at their posture, it was possible to discern what they were really thinking. If you learn how to use body language to your advantage, people will trust you and be more likely to believe you. You can achieve success in your relationships and career.

Let's have a look at the most common positions that contribute towards your body language.

Sitting positions

People don't realize how their posture can affect how they feel, or how they are feeling. It can be a sign of insecurity or shyness, or it can make you more confident and even aggressive. Let's have a look at these positions.

The Cross-Legged Position

It is a sign of carefree, openness and freedom to sit cross-legged. Crossing your legs with the knees extended to the side of the knees can give the subconscious illusion that you are willing to try new ideas. This can also subconsciously be perceived as a sign that you are also open to learning new things emotionally. Being open shows that you are a person who is fun and interesting, which can lead to more people being drawn to you.

The Erect Sitting Position

It's not difficult to see that a person who is comfortable in this position is confident, reliable and secure. If you do this all the time, whether you are conscious or unconscious, others will view you as this person. This is important, especially when it involves doing business. This is because people trust you more when you seem trustworthy and secure.

The reclined sitting position

This one is probably the best for Big Bang Theory, or an analytical, sitting position. Leaning forward is a sign that you're able and able to observe and think through situations without having the urge to immediately act. This shows that you might be more objective and able to look at a situation and think about it before acting. In a relationship perspective, this can help others see you as someone who cares deeply about others.

Crossed Ankle Sitting Place

It is common for people to sit with their feet crossed. This position gives off the impression that the person is not only elegant and refined, but also humble. This position can be paired with slightly bare legs to convey a sense that you are comfortable under your skin as well.

Clutching arms Sitting Position

You can't sit straight and hold onto the chair's armrests. This shows awareness and sensitivity.

It is possible to give a very different impression by just resting your arms on the chair and not clutching to it. Doing so communicates stability - physically, emotionally, and mentally. This is why people will often depend on you to provide their emotional and mental stability. They'll most likely see you as their figurative armrests.

Crossed-arm Sitting Position

Crossed arms often indicate confidence, strength, and defensiveness. It can also be an indicator that you are closed to new ideas. Crossing arms in front or behind the body can be taken to indicate protection of your body from the outside world. In either case, a crossed arm sitting posture is body language that suggests that a person does not feel weak or open.

Sidesaddle Sitting Position

This is for you, lady. Sidesaddle is a sitting position that allows you to place your knees on the sides. This sitting position can communicate a warm, caring, and gentle personality. Make sure you choose wisely whom you'll show the particular body position. The subconscious can interpret this as someone being open and willing to try something new (i.e., a relationship).

Hands on the Lap Sitting Position

If your hands are still and rest on your thighs, it could be interpreted as a sign of your shyness and thoughtfulness. If you can keep your hands still while sitting, you may come off as calm and collected.

Dead Center Sitting Position

Sitting comfortably on a couch, bench, and table communicates to other people that you are confident. Why? It's because people who lack confidence, i.e. are insecure or even tentative tend to fuss about where they sit. For most, sitting in the middle is uncomfortable. By sitting in a middle position, you signal to others that there is no need to be the center, and that you are comfortable with being anywhere.

Legs on Chair Arm Sitting Pose

This sitting position is mostly used by men because it involves the use of spread legs. This sitting position allows a person to stake his ownership and communicates an assertive and informal attitude.

While it's quite common to see two friends sitting down and having fun, this is not the right position for serious situations. Imagine that you're a boss who has just made a huge mistake at work and your subordinate approaches you. It's completely acceptable with you. If your subordinate feels awful about the mistake, he may sit down at your desk with his head held low and his hands on each knee. This is submissive body-language. After listening to what your subordinate says, you will quickly change to a sitting position on your chair. Your subtly communicating with your subordinate that your attention is not on his feelings and that you don't waste your time, by doing this you are saying that you don't give a damn about what he's feeling. It's like you're telling him the same story over and over again. This can be seen as dismissing subordinate's feelings.

This could be the reason why you are dismissing your subordinates' feelings. Maybe it's because you don't believe he has done anything seriously wrong, and that he shouldn't feel any shame about his error. Even if your subordinate doesn't understand what you mean, perhaps it's because you know how powerful body communication can be in communicating with others. Therefore, even if you meant well and really wanted to encourage him, your body language, i.e., the legs-on-the-chair-arm position, essentially communicates a vastly different message; one that aggressively says you're not interested in how he feels and that he's just wasting your time.

For your own sake, avoid using body language. In a business setting, this could cause you to offend your counterparts. It will also reduce your chances to negotiate successfully with them.

If another person takes this stance during business or professional meetings, it's an indicator that they don't value you as a person and believe they can get away with anything. Unless you reply accordingly. How can you do this without appearing angry or disruptive?

You can try to be funny but in an indirect way to tell him that you notice that he is doing this position. You might joke about telling him that his pants have fallen between his legs. If he does return to the same position, continue to break it in a subtle manner and, if necessary, a humorous way.

The Chair Straddling Sitting Pose

In the past, shields protected against enemy weapons. Today people will use any means available to show their protection against physical and verbal attacks.

If a person is able to symbolically guard himself or herself with a chair's support, they can also be able to straddle a chair. Additionally, such a position can make an individual appear dominant or aggressive, which can be helpful in fending off "attackers." Straddling a seat requires you to have your legs spread, so it can make you appear more assertive.

The chances of meeting a straddler are high that they are a person with a domineering personality. They love controlling others, and they can be very discreet. How do you approach a straddler? You can take back the power and convince them to change their ways.

As with all dominating positions, it is important to alter your position so that others are forced into theirs. By standing up, you can force your straddler to get out of the way and move to your side. You also have the chance of this work. If you stand behind the strangler, you force him orher to move in a way that he or she can't cover his back. This is something that strong personalities don't like.

What if the strangler is sitting on a swivel stool that can easily be turned around? Moving into your straddler's personal space is a way to challenge his or her perception of dominance. If you stand up to continue speaking with a stranger, it will place you in an awkward position where you can look down on them. However, moving into someone's space will make it much more difficult for them to continue straddling their chair. This will ultimately force them to give up the straddling position and find something more comfortable. Standing positions

Standing up, the legs, feet, and ankles do the bulk of the work. Legs and feet can be an excellent source of information, regardless of whether you are talking about yourself or others. But how can this be?

William Friesen as well as Dr. Paul Ekman conducted researches to determine deceptive behaviors. The research revealed that those who lie tends to reveal more through lower body movements. This is regardless of gender. This seems to be related to our awareness of movements, or lack thereof. People are generally more aware and conscious of their upper-body movements and gestures but not as much of the lower parts. This may be due to the fact the legs and feet are often out of sight when people interact with one another. Therefore, most people can't control their lower body movements as well.

Knowing the meanings of common standings can help you communicate effectively to others.

The Parallel Stance Standing Position

This standing position, which is most often used by subordinates, is one where the legs are straightened and the feet are close to one another. This formal standing position is used to subconsciously communicate neutrality.

This standing position is also more unstable than the others. Your feet are too close together and you have a weaker standing foundation than your wider-stance ones.

This position is dangerous because you could easily be pushed off balance or caught unaware.

This is when people are neutral on a particular topic/situation, i.e., they're uncertain, tentative, or cautious.

Spread Legs - Standing Position

This standing position is normally taken by men and subconsciously or subtly signals a stable, resolute position. This position allows you to communicate to others that your strength and dominance are evident. You can stand straight with your legs straight. But this time, you have both feet spread out - usually wider than your shoulder width - and your bodyweight equally distributed between both of them.

It is a dominantly male position due to average height. This means that men are typically taller and have higher centers. However, men use it more than women because it highlights dominance through a virile style. One reason for this is that men tend to not wear skirts, making the spread legs standing position somewhat uncomfortable.

The spread legs standing position is not only a way to make others look at your positive side, it can also help you feel better about yourself in times of depression. This standing position, with your shoulders pulled back and your head high, will quickly make you feel more confident, positive, and optimistic about yourself.

Standing position for Foot Forward

This position of one leg in front and one foot forward can help you send subconscious messages to other people about which direction you want to travel or who is most interesting to you. You can use this subtle signal to let others know where you are going or who the most interesting person is in the group.

Standing with your legs crossed

In a crowd, observe people standing around you and look out for those with crossed arms or legs. I ask you to pay more attention to their distance from other people than to those with crossed arms or legs. It'll be clear that they place themselves farther away from other people than those whose arms or legs are open while standing. Closed legs signal that a person is more defensive than open. This is illustrated by crossed legs which appear to restrict access to the genital zone.

It is possible for someone to cross their legs or raise their arms while standing straight up. This communication is not meant to be defensive but rather to indicate that they are feeling cold. How can you determine this? First, determine the temperature. If it's very cold, it might be done to keep the body warm. Another way is to examine where the hands are. If they aren't tucked between the armpits, they may be cold. If the legs are straight, pressing against eachother, and stiff it's likely to be a defensive strategy.

Chapter 4: 5 Surprising Truths Concerning Body Language

Many misunderstandings concerning body language have been accumulated by television shows like Lie to Me. These 'experts' micro-analyze each and every detail, making it seem that they care more about making body language appear like a deep science than actually providing education. Here are some surprising truths about bodylanguage.

Experts can often be wrong and even absurd in their advice.

It is absurd that experts keep claiming facts that certain gestures have specific meanings. It's almost not like each human being can be the same. Gestures have a lot of ambiguity. They can mean a lot or little. If someone crosses his/her arms, it could mean they are defensive, and a bit off... or maybe they are just feeling the cold and want some warmth. Experts disagree that folding your arms means you are defensive and not attracted. One of my best memories was when I was with friends at a party and met a beautiful lady. We were having great conversations and showing each other signs of attraction. But, halfway through our conversation, my friend pulled away from me. He needed me to tell him that he could clearly see that she was not interested due to the fact she had her arms crossed during their interaction. I laughed as he talked in my ear and thought it was hilarious. Let's cut it short: he was incorrect.

However, don't be too harsh with these people. The misunderstanding often comes from the pressure of appearing authoritative and providing instant analyses. Combine these two elements and you will end up with the kind of rigid assertions which body language experts double down on. It can help to listen, as they may have some truth to the things that they say.

However it is important to take what they are saying with a pinch salt. You don't have to believe what they say, just because they don't mean it.

The face is not a good starting point to read body language.

By the time most people are grown up, they have become skilled at masking their feelings. We have spent many years learning how to communicate and make concessions. So we pretend to be immersed, and we smile when we feel something else.

We're not all perfect at performing these polite deceptions. You will never be able to stop a stray smile. Most of all, the face is a friendly mask that helps everyone get along.

Sometimes, our strongest feelings can be revealed through the eyes.

If you're an expert in body language, micro-expressions are easy to identify. These are quick leakages of genuine emotion that occur through the mask of the human face. These micro-expressions can be very brief and are only temporary. This is why it takes some effort to notice them. They typically only surface when you have a strong feeling or belief that contradicts what you are actually admitting. The genuine feeling you feel will come across your face and disappear.

Body language signals intention, not specific meaning.

Experts get this wrong all the time. Emotional intention is often what body language communicates and can be interpreted with great accuracy. Psychologists believe that emotions are expressed first in the body, and then later in the conscious mind. Nanoseconds later is what we mean by "later". Your body will notice when you are angry, impatient, hungry, or happy first and send them signals. By learning to read and interpret body language, you can become an expert at understanding others' intent rather than the specific meanings in their conscious minds.

You are better than any expert at picking up body language cues on people who are familiar to you

Your ability to read body language is a skill that is well-known to people you already know. Take a moment to reflect on this. Unless, of course, you are completely clueless and have no self-awareness whatsoever, you should know immediately when your fiancee or kid is angry, bored, stressed, or if the boss is demanding something be done. Many hours have been spent studying with people we already know. We can identify the signs at a distance of a mile.

Before we learn more about bodylanguage and read other non-verbal clues in body language, let us first get to know the basics of understanding bodylanguage.

How to Read Body Language

To begin our discussion on body language, we will learn about the feet.

Nonverbal Cues from the Feet

It may come as a surprise, but feet are the most accurate body part to reflect how a person thinks. It is vital that you look at the feet of people you interact with closely without being too critical.

This theory states that for millions of generations, the human feet (along with the legs) have been our main method of responding to threats in the environment. The brain wired the human body so that feet would respond first to any threat. Your feet initiate the fight/flight response.

Instead of looking at someone from their head, inspect them from their feet.

Feet Direction

The most predictable human nonverbal behavior is to turn towards people or things that interests us or that make us feel like we are interested in them. This is a common response that is almost automatic and is often used to indicate if another person is happy for you to see them or prefers to be alone.

People often speak to one another toe-toe when they are interacting. If they are constantly turning their heads away from each other, or moving their feet in an outwardly directed arc, you can rest assured they would rather be somewhere else.

Crossed Legs

Crossed feet, which is different from crossed arms are often a sign that you are comfortable. In reality, people rarely cross their legs when they feel uncomfortable. Comfortable people will only cross their legs if they are confident.

The brain theory we discussed earlier about brain wiring states that crossed legs make it harder to maintain balance while standing. This is why our limbic brain restricts us from crossing our legs if we feel safe.

Let us now turn our attention to our torso.

Chapter 5: Reading Body Movements

You have reached the point where it is possible to get technical about body movement. This will allow you to put all you have learned about people into practice. This chapter will cover the most important parts of your body and how to interpret them.

The Face

Our faces are constantly communicating information. Think of your face as a projector sharing what's inside with the world. To avoid misinterpretation of a face's message, you must be aware there are many myths.

Your ability to interpret facial expressions will depend on what ethnicity or cultural background you have. I want you not to misunderstand. To achieve that, you must look beyond what is popularly promoted. All of our faces have lines and wrinkles with varying thicknesses. It is obvious that people's faces transmit information. Are you able to identify that information?

Common sense suggests that people who are relaxed will have their facial muscles relax. This is also true for the opposite. Even if someone seems to be conveying a compelling emotion verbally, judging by their facial expressions, there isn't much intensity. What does this mean? What does that tell you? This can be easily noticed if you are more familiar with the person and their basic behavior. Your facial expressions can be used to express emotions such as happiness, sadness and anger.

Although facial expressions can have a double edge depending on their use, it's easy to read body language. It is easy to see the difference between happy, sad and depressed faces. In this example, the lesson here isn't to learn how to recognize faces. It's more about digging deeper into hidden messages and learning to see them. Many people can learn to disguise their emotions. They could be "faking" a smile or pretending that they are interested in you. If this happens, it is essential to understand how to identify their microexpressions. If someone's facial expressions are contrary to their feelings, you will see their true emotions in just a few seconds. These facial expressions last only a few seconds and are easy to miss.

Eyes and Eyebrows

We are often told that the eyes open to the soul. Is the truth in the majority of the information you get about eye movement? There are many myths that surround the eyes that we must address first. For a long period, it was believed that honesty was a constant trait and that if someone didn't look you in their eyes, it was a sign of deception. This is one of the many myths to look out for. As we have mentioned, each culture has its own customs about what level of eye contact is appropriate. You shouldn't be quick to judge someone who doesn't want to start you in the eyes when you're speaking to them. Instead of being biased, try these signals to get the message across.

Notice the Pupil.

Excited about something? The pupil will naturally dilate. But the reverse can also be true. If the person is offended or angry, the pupil will automatically shrink. Paying attention to the pupil's physical size and the various changes you see as you interact can help you determine how the other person is responding and whether you are keeping their focus.

The Eyebrows

Eyes and pupil aside, eyebrows can be used to communicate feelings. A woman's eyebrows that are raised can signify friendlessness and sometimes even submissiveness. There are so many selfies out there today that you can't help but take.

You'll notice that you tend to be more attractive to particular "looks". If you look closely, the reason may have to do with your eyes or eyebrows. Raised eyebrows, and lower eyelids can appear very attractive and suggestive. This is not an intimidating look. Lower eyebrows convey authority but are not dangerous. They convey authority and aggression. Low eyebrows combined with glaring blue eyes are a recipe for disaster.

How to Read People with Your Eyes

The first step in determining someone's baseline is to identify them. Everybody has their baseline. That is, how they behave under normal, benign conditions. This means you must spend some time with the person who you wish to read, and then casually talk about neutral topics that aren't likely to cause them to become defensive or lie. You can start with everyday routines like the weather. Once you are familiar with the baseline, it becomes easy to spot the clues which will tell you what is wrong. These clues include:

Squinting occurs when you don't like someone or something you're saying. It can signal suspicion unless the surroundings are dimly lit, in which case they might be trying to see more clearly. If someone stares at your face, you should take a few moments to speak directly with them and clarify your statements.

Eye blocking occurs when there is a covering or shielding of the eyes. Also, you may see a lot more blinking and/or eye rubbing. It's a powerful display that you are expressing disbelief, anger, or fear.

Eye direction is a key indicator of lying. Several studies suggest that someone who looks up at the right side is either imagining or lying. When they look leftward, they are likely to be remembering something using their brain's memory. Vanessa Van Edwards from the science and people shares a simple formula that everyone can follow.

Auditory Thought is to their right. This refers to the ability of the listener to remember a song.

Visual Thought can be seen to their right (e.g. recognizing the color of a gown).

You can see that someone is creating a feeling, or a sensory memory. (e.g. you are thinking of what it would look like to swim under jello).

To their left, someone is talking to herself or himself. [Source: scienceofpeople.com]

Mouth

Is important information also transmitted by the mouth? Absolutely. You can learn a lot by the way your lips are placed and used. There are many different ways to squeeze your lips together. These signals can be used in a number of ways. Although non-verbal communication is important for both men and woman, it might surprise you to learn that women often communicate more with their mouths rather than their lips.

Lips are actually part and parcel of our skin. They are delicate and thin. As you can see, animals have different lips to ours. Our lips seem very expressive and attractive. This is likely why they play a major role in sexual communication.

Consider the emotional act, of kissing. Aren't your lips able to tell you so much about your partner, just by a single kiss? Unconsciously, you can tell a great deal from a single kiss. That's an excellent example of nonverbal communication. It doesn't matter if you're kissing your lover, but there are other cues to look out for when you read someone's lips and mouth. These cues can come in handy when you have a conversation or if you want to talk to a woman.

A playful and cute gesture between lovers is to kiss their lips. It could be used to give a kiss, or to make it seem flirtatious.

Pouting – When the lower portion of your lip is moved forward. It is used to express anger and discontent.

Licking the lips. The meaning of this gesture can vary depending upon the context. To avoid confusion, make sure you fully understand what is going on to prevent misinterpretation. If it is sexual lick, it will indicate that the gesture is intentional. You start in the corner of your mouth, and move slowly to the lower lip. It indicates a desire. The nervous lick is another kind of lick. It is fast and short, often indicative of tension. People who self-lick may be trying to relieve pressure through self-soothing.

If you notice someone biting their lips nervously, this could be an indication that they are anxious or uneasy about something. Unless they are trying moisturize their lips or if it is a habit that they have developed during deep concentration.

You can use biting your lips (similar to licking) to communicate sexual desire. It could also be a form self-restraint. The person may try to hold back anger or thoughts.

One thing to keep in mind about all lip communication, is that it often signals sexual communication or tension control. We often touch or use our lips for stimulation and comfort.

Breathing

Knowing how fast, slow, deep, or shallow a person's breathing is can tell you a lot. You can tell how someone is breathing by their actions. These signals can help you identify what patterns in your breathing are.

Rapid and severe breathing

This could be a sign you are experiencing fatigue and/or fear. As the heart beats more quickly and the lungs receive more oxygen, your breath becomes heavy and rapid. It is almost like you need to catch breath. You may notice that someone seems to be "catching their breath". This could either be due to physical exertion (or fear).

Deep breath

It could be a sign that you are in love, attracted to, or excited, which can be intense positive emotions. Or, it could be anger or fear which can be equally intense on both the positive and negative sides of the spectrum. If you're attentive, deep breathing patterns are easy to detect. If you tell someone something, and they hold their breathe or take a deep inhale just before shouting out, then they are likely to have deep breathing patterns. Deep breathing can be seen when a guy wants to impress his girl. A guy might take a deep breathe in before going up to a girl to make his upper bodies appear wider. It can also make his abs seem smaller. This is usually attractive to the other sex.

Sigh:

Sighs usually communicate hopelessness and sadness. However, it is possible to use them to convey relief. People who are in the midst of a long struggle might sigh out to express their frustration and pray for relief.

Arms, Hands, And Fingers.

Let's discuss the various arm positions and what they could indicate.

The most basic and natural hand gesture is for your hands to be resting on the sides.

You can see that the hands are behind the head as a sign of authority and comfort. But it can also signal tension and anxiety. How can you tell which one is which. Take a few moments to look at the way your hands are wrapped around each others. You are more likely to be in a superior hand position if one hand is comfortably held in the palms of the other behind your back. In such a scenario, the person would seek to demonstrate his security and dominance in the context. An army instructor, a professor on a podium. If someone suddenly feels threatened by something/someone, they are more inclined to take a tight grip to "keep their head together", and if that becomes too much, change to folded arms.

People who put their hands in the pockets often think that this is something they are ashamed of, or are hiding something (like a bad habit of nail biting or fidgeting).

Legs and Feet

People don't pay enough attention to what their feet and legs are communicating with the rest of their bodies. You know, like when was it the last time you looked at where your feet were as you conversed with someone?

The reason we tend not to pay attention to our feet or legs is that they are the furthest from the brain. It prefers to focus only on the face because that's where the spotlight is. Paying more attention to the legs, and feet, is crucial if your goal is to read intent and communicate with people. You should take the time to look at how your legs work when you are standing. Do you notice the direction of where your feet point? Are they pointing in the right direction when you're having a business encounter? It changes when you have a relationship with someone intimate or social. How stable do your feet feel while standing?

Experts suggest that self-confidence is directly related to how one stands. Introverts are more likely to be close to their feet than others. This is a sign that the person is submissive and makes them smaller targets. It is easy for someone with such a stance to be thrown out, both socially as well. It's possible that your stance will be very narrow if you don't like drawing attention.

You will also be more confident and assertive if you want to make a statement and appear authoritative. If you have to place your feet in front someone, it can look intimidating and hostile. A more relaxed position is to place your weight on one of your feet and have the other point to the side. Let's examine some meanings you might get from different leg positions.

To form a Stork, a female gesture is to place one foot forward and the other behind her. Because males are more flexible than females, they use this defense mechanism more frequently. Although it is very easy for someone to become unstable, this can be done easily. If you notice this in your girl, be careful of your approach. Often, this is a signal of timidity or fear. Approach the situation with gentleness and care, as you would with a terrified animal.

Crossing of legs, while quite common, does NOT necessarily signify that the person has closed-minded. It is a myth. It depends on the context. You might ask someone to pee. It could be that they feel comfortable in that environment and are communicating that their current situation is tied up. A negative sign can only be seen if the outcome is suspicious and the person isn't willing to change his mind. They may not believe you if they are not convinced.

Happy feet are easy for people to notice because they are often excited. Just look at how "springy," a person's steps are to determine if they are walking on clouds nine. Happy people have jumpy strides. They seem almost ready to fly off the ground.

Chapter 6: Body Posture

You can communicate a lot about yourself by how you sit and move when you interact. If that seems a bit vague to you, think about this: Have ever you felt suspicious of someone who looks good, talks well, and smells nice. I don't mean the nice appearance. But, deep down, did you feel that someone may be trying something over you? While you may not be aware, it is possible to pick up on the body language of a person, including their body positions, subconsciously. By observing their postures, you can pick up on their inner thoughts on a subconscious level. If you learn how to use body language to your advantage you can easily persuade people and gain their trust. You will eventually find success in your relationships and career.

Let's have a look at the most common positions which contribute to body language.

Sitting position

Many people don't realize it, but how you sit can speak volumes about your mood or feelings. It can be a sign of insecurity or shyness, or it can make you more confident and even aggressive. Let's have a look at these positions.

The Cross-Legged Position

It is a sign of carefree, openness and freedom to sit cross-legged. Crossing your legs with the knees extended to the side of the legs can give people the subconscious impression that you're willing to try new ideas. This can also subconsciously be perceived as a sign that you're open to learning new things emotionally. Being open is a sign you're someone who's interesting and fun to be around, which can result in more people finding you attractive.

The Erect Sitting Position

It is obvious, even without really thinking about it, that a person who sits this way all the time is confident, reliable and secure. When people see you like this, they will also think so. This is a great trait to have, especially when dealing with business. This is because people trust you more if you feel trustworthy and secure.

The Reclined Sitting Position

This one is probably the best for Big Bang Theory, or an analytical, sitting position. Leaning forward is a sign that you're able observe and consider situations objectively without having too much to do with them. This shows that you might be more objective than other people and may be able separate yourself from a situation and consider it carefully before acting. From a relational perspective, it can give the impression of someone who is aware of others feelings which can help to build trust and loyalty.

Crossed Ankle Sitting Place

In most cases, the position of sitting with the ankles crossed doesn't give the impression that the person is not only elegant and refined, but also humble. This position can be paired with slightly opened legs. It conveys a feeling that one is comfortable in their own skin and in their surroundings.

Placing your feet on the back of the chair

Sitting stiffly and literally clutching at chair's arms shows awareness of surroundings. Clinging to armrests can cause a person to appear to be emotionally and physically unstable.

It is possible to give a very different impression by just resting your arms on the chair and not clutching to it. Doing this communicates stability - both emotionally and mentally. This is why people will often depend on you to provide their mental and emotional stability. You'll be their figurative armrests.

Crossed-arm Sitting Position

Crossed arms often indicate confidence, strength, and defensiveness. Crossed arms can also be interpreted as a sign that one is closed to new ideas. It could also be interpreted as a sign that one is protective of oneself. With arms crossed in front, one might interpret this as protecting one's body against the rest of the globe. In either case, a crossed-arm sitting posture is body language that suggests that the individual is neither weak nor open.

Sidesaddle Sitting Position

This is the one for you, if you're a girl. The sidesaddle position, where your knees are bent to the side, is an amazing sitting position. This sitting position conveys a natural sweet, caring, and delicate personality. This is why it's important to be careful about who you show your body position. It can also subconsciously signal that the person is open to exploring new possibilities.

Position of a hand-on lap sitting position

It could be interpreted as a sign of a thoughtful, shy person if your hands are resting on your thighs. If your hands can remain still while seated, it could indicate calmness and composure.

Dead Center Sitting Position

Sitting at the center of a chair, bench, or table communicates confidence to others. Why? It is because people who lack confidence, i.e. are insecure or tentative, tend to fret about where they should sit. Most of them find that sitting in the middle is uncomfortable. The idea behind sitting in a middle position is to communicate to others your confidence in being at the center.

Sitting Position: Legs on Chair Arm

This sitting position is mostly used by men because it involves the use of spread legs. This sitting position communicates an aggressive, informal and personal attitude.

While it is quite common to see two friends sitting down and having fun, this position is inappropriate for more serious situations. It could be that your boss has a subordinate who comes to you after making a mistake at work. You are perfectly happy with this. You say that your subordinate feels awful about the mistake. Now, he is sitting at your table with his head held low and his hands on the floor. This is submissive body-language. After listening to what your colleague has to say, you suddenly adopt a chair arm position. Your subordinate will know that you don't care much about how he feels, and you won't waste your time. It's like you're telling him that you're bored with the same old story. This is a way of dismissing subordinates' feelings.

This could be the reason why you are dismissing your subordinates' feelings. Maybe it is because you don't believe he has done anything wrong, and that he shouldn't feel sorry for his mistakes. Even if your subordinate doesn't understand what you mean, perhaps it's because you know how powerful body communication can be in communicating with others. Therefore, even if you meant well and really wanted to encourage him, your body language, i.e., the legs-on-the-chair-arm position, essentially communicates a vastly different message, one that aggressively says you're not interested in how he feels and that he's just wasting your time.

For your own sake, avoid using this body language. You might end up irritating your counterparts in a business setting. Your chances of being able negotiate successfully with them will be significantly reduced.

If you see someone taking this stance in a business, or professional, meeting, it means that they are thinking lowly of your abilities and think he can do whatever he wants with you. Unless you are prepared to respond. How can you do this without appearing angry or disruptive?

You could try to be funny and indirect and tell him that this is not the right way to do things. You could joke about telling him that his pants are too short or placing something near his body that'd force him to change the position. If he is still in the same position, continue to break it down in a subtle way and, if you can, make it funny.

The Chair Straddling Sitting Pose

It was common for men to use shields to protect themselves against the weapons of their enemies. People now use whatever symbol is available to show their protection against physical and verbal attacks. They may hide behind objects such as doors, gates or fences.

If a person is able to straddle a chair, it will symbolically allow him or her to defend themselves. The position can make an individual appear domineering and aggressive, which can be useful in fighting off "attackers". Straddling a Chair requires a spread of legs. It also makes it easier for a person to take up more space.

The chances of meeting a straddler are high that they have a domineering personality. They enjoy controlling others whenever they become bored. In most cases, they are very discreet. How can you approach a straddler? Give them power back and you will increase your chances of convincing him or she to change their mind.

As with all dominating positions, it is important to alter your position so that others are forced into theirs. By standing up, you can force your straddler to get out of the way and move to your side. This works well because the person behind you is in a vulnerable position. People with strong personalities are not fond of being in this position.

Now what if the strangler is sitting in a swivel chair? This can allow him to easily turn the chair around and not have to give up his or her straddling position. Moving into your straddler's personal space is a way to challenge his or her perception of dominance. If you stand up to continue speaking with a stranger, it will place you in an awkward position where you can look down on them or her. However, moving into someone's space will make it much more difficult for them or her to continue to straddle the chair. It will eventually force them or her to stop straddling and find something more comfortable.

Standing positions

When standing, the legs and feet do most the work. Therefore, they can be very useful in obtaining information about others and yourself. But how do you explain this?

William Friesen as well as Dr. Paul Ekman conducted research on deceitful behaviors. Their research revealed that people who lie tends to give off more signals via lower body movements, regardless if they are male or female. This seems to be related to a consciousness of actions, or lack thereof. People are generally more aware and conscious of their upper bodies and gestures but not as much of their lower body parts. This may be due to the fact the legs and feet are often out of sight for people when they interact with others. As such, people don't have the ability to control their lower body movements as well as their upper bodies.

Knowing the meanings of subconscious messages and common positions can help you communicate effectively with others.

The Parallel Stance Standing Position

This standing position, which is most often used by a subordinate, is when one stands with both legs straightening and the feet aligned with each other. This is a formal, standing position that can subconsciously convey a neutral outlook such as that of a child teacher when talking to the teacher, or an army man when addressing his commanding Officer.

This standing position is much more vulnerable than others. The feet closest to the ground while standing is a weaker foundation, compared with wider-stanced ones. This position is dangerous because you could easily fall off balance or be caught unprepared.

This is when people are usually neutral on a specific topic or situation.

Spread Legs Standing Position

The men usually take this standing position. This subtly, or subconsciously, communicates a stable and resolute posture. This position allows you to subtly communicate with others that you will hold your ground and demonstrate your dominance. You can stand with your legs straight. This time, you place your feet far apart.

It is a dominantly male position due to average height. This means that men are typically taller and therefore have higher centers. It is not limited to men's height. The genital area is used to highlight dominance in a virile way, which isn't the case with the ladies. One reason for this is that men tend to not wear skirts, making the spread legs standing position somewhat uncomfortable.

The spread legs standing position is not only a way to make others look at your positive side, it can also help you feel happier about yourself in times of low self-esteem. When you are standing with your shoulders back, your head raised, and your posture is relaxed, it will be a matter of seconds before your emotions change.

Standing position for Foot Forward

This position of one leg in front and one foot forward can help you send subconscious messages to other people about which direction you want to travel or which person is most interesting to you. You can use this subtle signal to let others know where you want to go and who the most interesting person is in your group.

Crossed legs Standing Position

In a crowd, I ask you to observe people standing around and look out for people who have crossed their arms or legs. I ask you to pay more attention to their distance from other people than to those with crossed arms or legs. You will find they are closer to other people than those whose arms or legs are open when standing. If someone has closed legs, it is indicative of a defensive or closed mindset. The crossed legs which appear to prevent access to the genital zone can signify this.

There's a chance that someone crossing their legs or arms while standing up does not mean that they are defensive, but that they feel cold. So, how did you find out? First, measure the temperature. If the temperature is low, it might be done to keep warm. Another way to check where your hands are located is to place them in a mirror. If they're not tucked between the armpits they will be cold. If the legs are straight and press hard against one another, they're likely trying to keep warm.

Chapter 7: Head Action

Its movements and gestures can give meaning to the character's motives and feelings. It is similar to the gestures in the arms or hands but has a different non-verbal language. Sometimes it can be unclear and subtler. An actor's ability to recognize the potential for these gestures and understand their implications is invaluable, especially in film acting when the head and facial images dominate the screen.

Head gestures let people communicate a variety thoughts and feelings. However, head movements alone are not capable of conveying as much detail as words. They can have many meanings and are open for interpretation. In many cases the context of the scene and relationships will determine the implications of the gesture. As such, head gestures often enhance or accent the dramatization of other choices.

There are many motions available for the head. These include tilt, tilt, slant and any combination thereof. They can also be performed with varying quality, from subtle to dramatic, from fluid and frantic to exaggerated. Another reason is their relationships to other acting entities. This includes dialogue, facial expressions, body movements and body movements. Are they in sync with, following, or preceding these entities' actions? What do they say about the other entities? Explore these aspects with various examples so you can better understand both the limits as well as the potential of head gestures.

Let's examine the most familiar gestures. The nod of one's head and tilting the head in an upward or downward direction indicates acceptance, acknowledgment, or agreement. It could also indicate "Yes." The headshake, where the head turns from side-to-side, can often be used as a sign of "no." It is used most often to express a negative reaction, or to indicate disagreement. These meanings of the nod and the head shake are universally accepted. But, some countries have other meanings. Depending on the context, a side-to-side tilting in arcs of the head may be used in South Asian cultures such as India to indicate "Yes," the "Good," the "OK" or the "I Understand" meaning.

The head toss could refer to several things like "Get out", "It's above there," or, "Shutup, the boss just entered." This gesture is common in group situations where a cryptic message needs to be sent. The head tossing gesture is usually subversive. It's directed at one person, and it signals a need to act. It is important to make eye contact when completing the transaction.

One interpretation of the head roll is "I don't know", "What could that possibly be" or "Why are they asking me?" The gesture helps to avoid an issue. It is directed away of the confronting person/entity. This interpretation includes the eyes looking at devoid areas and their sight lines.

The cutoff is closely related with the head roll, in that it suggests uncertainty or separation. This gesture is when the head turns away or avoids direct eye contact from the person confronting you. The gaze can reflect an insecurity or disagreement. Perhaps the eyes are searching for answers and making subtle comments about the confronting individual. The cut-off provides an opportunity for unencumbered internalizations. There is no one watching. The blocking move allows for another perspective, which can either be truthful or deceitful.

Head tilt could indicate contempt or a judgmental pose. You can further define this gesture by the accompanying facial expression. For example, flared nostrils could indicate contempt, or squinting gazes for a judgemental pose. The eyes help to define the target, and can be adjusted for intensity to maintain interest. The gesture should be sustained for the right impact. But if the gesture is too long it can make the scene look forced, which can result in the scene losing its integrity.

Side slant with the forehead pointing to one side may indicate compassion, interest, or even skepticism. Combine this with looking intently, and interest is even more obvious. A sympathetic expression and a downward tilt are signs of compassion. Side slants are accompanied by a slight upward angle and probing eyes.

There are many applications for the Head Swivel. It can indicate the character's thinking or speech by the direction and goal of the head twist. In these cases, the "what," could be something tangible like objects or people. They can also be imagined entities. A head turn, combined with eye behavior, takes us to that space. We are able to see and feel what the character envisions. The head-swivel is used for scanning new environments and observing them. Another use is when two people converse side-by-side. The head swivel allows them to acknowledge and/or comment on what has been said. This subtle interaction can lead to a very productive exchange when it is combined with eye behaviour. This is possible because both behaviors are available to the audience. Therefore, ideas, thoughts, reflections and physical relationships become more important.

The head tilt is used to look aways and detach yourself from the person you're talking to. These areas include the following: Comfort area, problem area recall, avoidance and avoidance zones. These areas combine head turns and eye behavior. They help to delineate areas that are of concern, clarify inner thoughts and feelings.

Around Corner. The head moves around to improve the angle of a character's vision when it is blocked by something. This movement involves the upper body moving up or sideways to improve your view. This movement shows a stronger commitment to interest than the side angle and enhances the impact. This move can be made by the upper body only moving sideways, or together with the head-slant. The first version is comical while the latter is more authentic.

Use emphatic gestures of the head to create strong convictions. Such movements, typically up and down and in a rhythmic fashion, punctuate and highlight dialogue. These movements often go along with the rhythms and phasings of the words. But, if the effect is repeated too often, it becomes redundant and loses its power. This gesture can be used in scenes with high-powered speeches or confrontational arguments if it's done well.

Leaning in can be a sign you are paying attention, interested or desirous. This subtle head movement is almost imperceptible and can be very telling about a person's feelings. It means that the person listening is being heard. It is a sign of a connection. With the right facial expressions or eye behavior, the viewer will sense what is being communicated nonverbally. If the guy is looking longingly at his lips, then it could indicate the emotion desire.

A person who leans back may be disinterested, skeptical, or cautious. This behavior is usually more perceptible and reactive. Something has changed the character's mood, such a boring subject, precarious situations, or worrisome proposition. The movement indicates survival and a wait-and see attitude. It could be an abrupt sign that there is a scary or alarming event. If so, you might need to take action and flee the scene.

The Head Shrug could have several meanings. It could indicate "I don't understand", "I have no idea", "I'm not interested," "So what," and "Whatever."

This movement elevates the shoulders to decrease the neck. A slanted head can give the gesture a more welcoming dimension. This gesture is often used in combination of dialogue. If you do, it's best to put it in place before the dialogue. This approach follows a feel-think-act speak sequence. It is considered to be the most sincere. The overall effect of the gesture when used in dialogue is weaker. The gesture may be implied as an insincere response, intimidation, or reaction if it is used after the dialogue. This gesture could also be used as an afterthought.

The Head Dip describes a state that is often associated with being tired, grieving, or thinking about an idea or problem. The Head Dip allows the character to reach a state of comfort by lowering their heads. As with all gestures; the juxtaposition of scene context, dialogue, or facial expressions can affect the way one perceives the nonverbal entity.

The Crumble is an example of a reactionary head movement and is common in dramatic situations. The gesture combines the leaning in and a subtle upward and downward quiver of your head as you move forward. It's a sign of hope, relief and sometimes grief. It is also called the crumble, as the character is almost breaking down as it dribbles forward. Its vulnerability is very evident. This gesture is an internalization or visualization of thoughts and emotions.

Head gestures include the alignment of the eyes and nose. When conveying emotions such a suspicion or jealousy, the eyes respond more quickly than the head. In contrast, when emotions such as curiosity, desire, and jealousy are involved, the eye/nose angle becomes more aligned. In fearful situations, however, the eye/nose angle can be more aligned. It can also be used for non-confrontational anger or disdain by using an acute eye/nose angles.

Stillness can be used as a head gesture. Minimal movements signify many great things. It allows the eyes to shine and facial expressions can take center stage. It creates tension, vulnerability and increases tension. In motionlessness, viewers are allowed to look inside the characters heads and wonder what is going on. It also allows for audience collaboration to speculate about what's to come next.

Overuse of head gestures is the most common fault. As with all gestures, repeated use can wear away the effect and cause it to lose its effectiveness. Instead, focus on key moments in your story that will allow you to use gestures to support the characters emotions and intentions. Instead of repeating dialogue content, search for hidden facts to reveal the true essence. Use gestures to reveal what's happening.

Another flaw in the scene is being too opaque and too on point. These gestures, which are clearly noticeable and hinder the integrity the scene, stand out as distinct from the performance. Sometimes this is due not to portray the acting style correctly. A comic style's behavior is exaggerated, more precise, and easier to read. In dramas, the behavior is more credible with implied meanings and is balanced by external and internal forces.

One common mistake, especially among beginners, is to be too mechanical. This flaw is often corrected by practicing head gestures in varying intensities at various speeds. You should learn how to control your timing, dynamics, and qualities. This will help you portray more authentic scenes.

The dancing head flaw is when the head gyrates. This is often an innate behavior, which the actor isn't aware of. When the actor is required for rehearsals with a book on their heads, it becomes obvious that this is a dancing head.

Others. These attributes can include attitudes, opinions, or social status. An example of this is an amicable attitude. It will also be more open to other ideas and more accommodating. Contrary to the friendly stance of a Liberal, someone with conservative views could be more uppity. Social status can also be seen in the lower head of a suppressed worker as compared to the confident head-high position of a CEO.

Another factor that influences the size and impact of movements is how large the head is in the frame. For visual impact to have an effect, the movements should be larger than the head in a long view. Because they will appear more powerful and quicker in close ups, subtle movements are better. The same logic applies on a stage for theater. It is important that gestures are readable to the back of the seats.

Contradictions of head gestures and acting choices are not common. Gestures are used to communicate truth. However, dialogue, facial expressions and blocking can all be used to hide the truth. Con artists and untrustworthy characters sometimes fall for con artists' truthful gestures that mask a falsehood in other areas. This dissonance creates a richer character that draws the reader into the story. Deceitful gestures might be used by a call girl to get money from a client. These contradictions add depth and color to the characters, making them more captivating.

It is better to make your movements and gestures stand out, and make them easily readable. They should be in tune with the story and compatible with the character or his/her relationships.

Writing about nonverbal entities is more difficult when written in a literary format. Gestures don't have words; they are gestures that communicate an idea or convey a feeling. You can visualize these gestures by seeing them in motion. These gestures will appear more natural and authentic if you can see them in motion. It is essential to present gestures in an authentic and natural way, as with all aspects acting. This can happen through focused training and extensive practice until gestures become an integral part the character's behavior.

As we have already mentioned, head gestures can take on many meanings depending on the context. While this book can explore some of these meanings, it cannot cover all the possibilities. Explore these options and learn more about this topic on your personal journey. This article outlines the best methods to help you absorb these techniques. Your research will reveal the importance of using gestures and movements to convey the story.

Chapter 8: Body Language for Seduction

Because we are social animals, we have a history using non-verbal messages to communicate messages. They are most effective when we are showing our interest in others and when we want to unite our interest. Since people are exploiting body language as a means of seduction to prey upon others, this idea has become more complicated. Even though there are many ancient skills that you can use to make others happy, it is possible to achieve amazing results with them. It doesn't just involve attracting the other sex on same-sex. It depends on the intent or orientation of the individual. The goal of seduction is to draw others towards you and what you do. It also involves changing your perception of how things work. The ability to attract others' attention allows one to have total control of the relationship.

The power game that is seduction can be tempting. It allows men and women to pursue their own goals, regardless of whether they are achieving the same goals. Only the top players can take control of each other in this game. How can you convince? It all depends on how one conveys their message and how they are conceived by their audience. For example, women might desire to seduce a man who is wealthy to make him feel financially comfortable. A singer may have a tendency to seduce people with charm and wit when selling his or her music. To win the office of his choice, a politician may use all kinds of seduction tactics. You must have a plan in place to achieve the desired results.

Seduction means to persuade, manipulate, or lead astray someone's mind to gain full control over their emotions, perceptions, thinking, and feelings. It can be negative or positive, depending on the motive. Seduction can be used in a positive way to seduce people, either to obtain something or to keep them from their deceits. But it should always be done ethically. However, seduction can be used in a manipulative way to induce people to do things that they would not under normal circumstances. A deceitful technique may include using a threat to induce acceptance or manipulative to conceal the past wrong they have done.

How does Body Language seduction occur?

This can be done in a practical manner for better understanding. You could, for instance, drop something onto the flow in front people in the group or class and then bend down so you can pick. What is the reaction of those around you to this? Is it possible to see how many people look at you when you pick up the staff? People generally notice the movement of others around them. People will pay more attention to the first movement of your body. They will watch you as you move on and, if you don't answer their questions immediately, they will go back to their old routine. You can minimize the impact of body motion by this. You might also consider moving your body or bending. This may surprise you even more about how they react.

If possible, mirror yourself as you try to seduce someone. When she crosses her legs, you do the following: Try to copy what she does by raising her head or extending her hand. It's like making an acquaintance with the other person just by copying the actions of the other person. The other person is more likely to pick non-verbal clues than you and will be drawn to what you do. Because they have mutual understanding, both of them will be more comfortable working together. You can make the girl feel attractive by matching the body language or doing the same signs. They may like you for the responsiveness they show. They perceive you in a way that mirrors their feelings. Furthermore, getting to get to know each other doesn't just involve knowing their names. While mirroring each other's intentions may sound vague at first, both can benefit from putting all of their efforts into practice.

It's easier to convey the message properly if one makes the intention clear to the prey. To make it practical and effective, the target should be able to understand the body language. The key to seducing someone is to walk in close proximity to them. If this doesn't work, keep bumping into them more often in order to develop familiarity. If you are trying to seduce someone, they will more likely recognize familiar faces than strange ones. People will recognize you immediately if they have had an interaction before your familiar intent. Although they may not immediately recognize you, with persistence, they will likely recognize what your intentions are. Use fear to your advantage. Talk small about breaking the ice. This will reduce the feeling that you are a stranger. When you do that, they will likely be open to talking and you'll never know what you have in common with them. If she is the kind of girl you are looking for, now is the best time.

It is someone who regularly sees you and becomes more interested in you. It is a familiarity that breeds interest in each other. We are human beings. Social beings with feelings. It is sometimes more difficult to hide what we feel inside. Sometimes we long for that one person that we can share our feelings with, someone we can talk to without fear of discrimination or being judged. Sometimes strangers present an opportunity that we cannot avoid. All that is required is to follow the flow and accept their advancement as a way to feel the comfort of being wanted. Is it possible to deny or decline to be with someone who would love to have you in their life once in a while? You never know when that golden opportunity may come along again. Make the most of every opportunity and then wait for good things to happen. Patience pays, and patience is wise when you're looking for something serious.

It is possible to initiate the art or seduction simply by accidentally touching someone you wish to seduce. Even though it may seem difficult to get along with someone, the magic touch will make them notice you and realize your interest in them. You can touch someone even while exchanging goods or holding hands, while also greeting them as a friend. This will help to establish rapport and make it easier for the other person to understand your intentions. It is particularly useful for seducing a woman you have identified as a potential partner or spouse. While this technique may not work in every country it is only applicable in countries where touching in public is uncommon or people are not accustomed to the act. This is why creating the impression at the right time, the right place, and clearly stating your intent are key factors in making the game top-notch.

The touching technique is more powerful than body language. Research has shown that waitresses using this technique to hand out bills to guests at hotels receive a larger portion of the tip. Even more interesting is the fact that many customers do not know this technique exists and how it can cause them financial problems. If they knew the waitress had nothing to with them other than money, they would not be willing to take part in or allow themselves to be complicit in this act. They don't want to give the wrong tip because they are unable to distinguish between the right impression and the wrong impression. The body language is at its highest point and the waitress is so skilled in it that they are unable to let go. It's a buyer to seller transaction, although the customer is required to pay a fee to experience the imaginary pleasure.

Another study showed that the cashier at a shop tends to touch customers while they are making transactions or purchasing merchandise. Customers are attracted to this gesture because it is a pleasant gesture. However, the cashier making no attempt to touch the customer's hands while they are paying for merchandise will not be recognized as there has been no interaction on their part. They are considered just like any other shopkeeper, who is simply trying to make ends meet. One may ask what touch has on someone's attitudes about buying from you.

Touch is usually magical. It causes the body to react in ways people are unable to recognize. The connection made by touch allows one to feel connected and is seen as an act of acceptance. The feeling of being desired by the person who touches one makes one happy and lively about the situation. What will it feel like to be valued, appreciated, and respected by the person you are interacting with? How will the feeling you get from being accepted for the person you are, and how will it affect your life? In this case, the first person seems to care more for the customers than he does the second. That is why he may prefer to transact with him.

It is possible to apply the same technique in relationship seduction when the candidate initiates the conversation via touch. This technique is designed to get the attention the woman you plan to seduce. If the touch is done on a person, or towards prey species, it creates a positive feeling.

To seduce their prey, they will often make an exotic appearance. Surprise people can sense your eccentricity and make them feel more comfortable with you. This is the act of master of seduction. It clearly describes how to draw attention to the ceremony. People who are present at the party will not forget these memorable scenes. This technique is often used by the women to make a lasting impression on their potential husbands or boyfriends. Imagine sitting in bar with a woman dressed in a seductive garment that reveals a portion their bodies. The intention of the woman at the counter may not be evident to them, as she may not have intended that someone is there. To the person looking at the counter, however, the body language of a woman can cause them to feel attracted towards the woman who just walked into the bar.

Always be confident and graceful when walking if you are a man looking to seduce women. You can feel confident by maintaining a straight back, shoulder taut, and not bending forward or backward. While eye contact is essential in the seduction process, it's important to keep in mind that stiff or rigid eye contact can create an intimidating impression. Make eye contact when seducing someone. This is an amazing tool that can help you get your man, but it can also cause problems. Eye contact is a key to finding a spouse or husband. Research has shown that seducers are more successful at looking at the camera than non-seducers in a study. Eye contact is a valuable non-verbal communication skill and can be useful in every conversation. Remember that eyes are the window of the soul. With the right eye contact, you can see the depths of your soul.

Importantly, those who are skilled at seduction have a natural ability to use facial expressions to convey their feelings and intentions. It's evident that facial expressions have a positive effect on seduction. Make sure your facial expression matches your feelings if you intend to seduce her. You want to show a woman that your true feelings are valued and not just to impress them. Nobody will want to be around a joker, or someone who isn't serious with them. Someone who is trying to play with their emotions for their pleasure and satisfaction. A good seducer will usually use tricks with their mouths, and how they use the mouth to impress the other party. A subtle smile, with a short lips lick expression, can make a lady more interested in you. You can either get the feeling that they are interested or you like their style, and she will lick your lips. Be subtle. It's important not to make it too obvious. Any overdoing can often make a false impression on the target prey. In this instance, the man/woman you are interested is.

How do we smell? How does it affect seduction? Yes, it is. How you will feel when you encounter someone who is sweaty all over the body matters. How do you feel when you interact with such people? Also, how does it feel to get wet and hug someone in the street? Do you feel confident in your abilities or are you just unable to do the things you must? The best method for seducing women is to have a good smell. When you approach that woman you admire from the side, put on a pleasant fragrance and cologne. The majority of women will be interested in knowing what type of perfume you are using. Men can use this opportunity to make the talk you fear most. You can make your body smell amazing and they will love you. Is it possible to want to be loved by someone other than your preference if you aren't normal or attracted towards the same sex?

It is possible to incorporate the tone and facial expression into the seduction process. In most cases, people will use their non-verbal communication skills well until they are unable to communicate. Your communication skills are very important in the seduction process. This technique, if not properly used, can lead to serious issues. Imagine yourself struggling with other techniques only to find that your tonal voices are dictating your actions. How will it feel to have this happen to you. It's likely you wont feel happy about it. The funny thing is, you might not realize it until after you are done. While the other person will not be able to tell you, the reactions and how they react to you after the whole affair will let you know that your tone was off. It is crucial to choose the right tone for seduction. The other person will feel positive if your tone is soft and pleasant. Your tone alone will likely get a woman talking to you. However, being harsh and negative can cause withdrawal and irritation for the other side. It is possible to ruin the mood you created with your non-verbal communication skills while seducing someone by using harsh words. In order to have a lasting relationship, you must maintain the correct tone at all times.

Chapter 9: Trust Your Intelligence

Your intuition, also known as your instinct, can know more than you might think. This inner compass can detect information in situations that your conscious brain may not have. We are often trained to ignore this inner part of us, but it is possible to regain that connection by trusting our intuition regularly and using it.

Researchers and psychologists believe our instincts and intuitions are so powerful, because they read information that our conscious mind is not able to. In a second, you can process more information than 11,000,000. Your conscious brain doesn't have enough time to read through all that information. So it focuses only on what is pertinent to you at this moment. Your conscious awareness focuses on what you have chosen. You may not be aware of all these things, but that does not mean they no longer exist. Your brain continues to absorb all of this information. Your subconscious mind is still sorting through all the information to help you understand it all. If it finds an important thing, it will raise that consciousness to your conscious awareness. If it does no feel the need, or doesn't have enough information to raise it up to your conscious awareness it will feed that information into your intuition. So, you have those "gut feelings", about different situations, places, people.

Your intuition is not something you should overthink

Your intuition is an intuitive judge of character. It can often be more accurate than your logic. But if you think too much about your intuition, or any information you perceive through your intuition, it can lead to inaccuracies. The best way to judge a person using your intuition is to trust what you feel about them or what you have based on their first impression.

Watching someone is a great way to learn about their body language and facial expressions. You will instantly notice if they seem trustworthy, whether their emotions drive their words, or what thoughts they may have.

Avoid Attaching To Intuitive Beliefs

Though intuition can give you great insight into a situation and provide valuable information, it is not wise to stick to your intuition beliefs especially when new information is provided. It's unhelpful, for example, to attach yourself to the belief that someone wants to do things with you, even if they tell you otherwise. Attaching too much to your beliefs can cause you to be disconnected from reality and can create unfavorable or unfair situations between people.

People can attach quickly to their intuitive beliefs by dreaming. If a person dreams about something, it can make them believe their dream is true. Imagine a person dreaming about a plane wreck and cancelling their vacation plans. In this scenario, they believe that their dream is real and that their intuition warns them to stay away from the vacation.

Another way people may do this is to believe that something is true and then feel anxious. It is possible to get the feeling that someone is harshly reviewing you. That feeling could lead you to feeling anxious and scared. You might try to change something or change your beliefs to make them agree with you. If they are not really harshly judging, or you have misinterpreted their signals then you might be wasting time and creating uncomfortable social experiences. Trust that people will be honest with you about your feelings and intuition. You do not have to force anyone to speak up for their feelings. Respect their right for silence and keep your attention on yourself.

Practice makes you more intuitive

Practice can help improve your intuition. You can improve your intuition simply by listening more to what it says and trusting its feelings. If you find yourself in a room, and your intuition tells, you can trust it to direct you out of the space. Even though you might not understand, the reasoning may never be known to you. But, by trusting your intuition, you are strengthening it and encouraging its support.

One way to increase your intuition, which can directly assist you in analysing people, is to stop thinking and let your intuition work. If you're constantly thinking about everything that you can rationally and reasonably believe you know, you could be drowning your intuition out. To clear your mind, observe someone and then ask your intuition to give you feedback. Read the feedback to understand what your intuition says.

Insight Is Seeing, Intuition Is Sensing

It is important you understand that intuition, insight, and insight are two different things. Intuition suggests that you have seen something. This could be the person's behavior or the knowledge that will help you understand their behaviour. However, intuition can be used to detect what another person is thinking and feeling. Sometimes, you may be able see the reason behind their actions. However intuition is a feeling, or a gut reaction. This is not a guarantee.

Effectively using your intuition, such as when analyzing people, is possible by allowing your intuition draw you to a conclusion. You then need to use logic and reasoning in order to validate your conclusion. If you feel that someone was misinterpreted by your intuition, you may use your intuition and gain more insight. But you shouldn't assume that your insight will be correct. Trust your intuition. However, you must be open-minded to seek out additional information to validate your findings.

Intuition wins over stress

Your intuition will give you the information you need to get through any stressful situation. Your intuition can guide you through troubled situations in a way that is safe and effective. If you are feeling stressed, your intuition will tell you some things about your friends and family.

However, your intuition can be less strong when you're feeling sad. When you feel sad, your intuition may be drowned by a voice inside your head that makes it worse. Although it may pretend it is your intuition it is not. You'll be told that everything is wrong, you don't have anyone to love you and there is no hope. You can tell it is not your intuition as it sends you messages of hopelessness, defeat and directions on how to get from this situation.

Don't trust your intuition if you feel sad or down. It could cause you false information to be trusted and make it harder to really understand the other person. Instead, try to rely more on practical measures, such as reading their body language or facial expressions.

You can read through the writings of others to get a sense of their personalities

The best way to learn about people is through their writing. Social media is everywhere these days. People post about their lives, thoughts and feelings on the internet. Surprisingly, you can see the writings of others and gain insights into their lives and experiences. Similar to seeing darting eyes or pressed cheeks or raised lips, you can learn a lot about someone by what they write, their punctuation, grammar, tone, and how they communicate.

They use cues when they write emails, social media posts or streams of consciousness, blog entries, or other online content. These cues are used to indicate who and what they're communicating. It is important to pay attention to the language they use. People who swear a lot often indicate they are probably highly neurotic, have poor conscientiousness, and will not accept help from others. It is easy to assume the same if they use words or phrases that indicate anger. This is an indication that they are depressed. If they speak in the past tense, it can also be assumed that they are depressed.

An online profile can be a great way to assess someone's character. What username do they use for their profile? What is their profile image? What has their bio said about them? The way someone has created their profile, and the words they used, can tell you if they're friendly, funky, funny, professional, angry.

Examining people's profiles on social networks is a great place to exercise your intuition. Spend time looking at profiles to see what kind of personality they have. Go through each profile carefully and let your intuition guide the way to the right conclusion about who this person is. If you can, look at their posts to confirm your assumption.

Chapter 10: Different Physical Movements

Covering your mouth could indicate that you are trying to suppress feelings and maybe even uncertainty. This could also suggest that they are thinking very hard and are uncertain of what next to say.

What you communicate with your body language or nonverbal signs can impact how others view you. It also impacts how they perceive you, what they think of you, and how trustable they are. Unfortunately, many people send negative and confusing nonverbal signals to others without knowing. This damages trust and connects people.

Subcategories

Oculesics

Oculesics is one subcategory under body language. This study focuses on eye movement and eye behavior. Oculesics is an area of nonverbal communication which uses eye behavior as a means to communicate meaning. Oculesics relies on cultural factors. To take an example from traditional Anglo-Saxon culture: Avoiding eye contact can be interpreted as a lack of confidence, certainty, truthfulness, or trust. However, direct or prolonged contact with an individual in Latino culture can be interpreted as a challenge to the person or a romantic interest. A lot of Asian cultures may consider prolonged eye contact a sign to be angry or aggressive.

Haptics

Haptics, which is a subcategory under Body Language, studies the use of touch in communication. As such, handshakes can have meaning.

Based on the Body Language Project data, touching is our most developed sense at birth. Touching is a way to soothe, have fun, communicate power and build bonds with others, such as baby and mother. Touching can communicate different emotions and the intensity. Touching that doesn't include other cues, such as length or type, can communicate anger, fear (or disgust), love, gratefulness, sympathy, and even hate. The length and place of touching can affect the meaning of the touch.

Studies have also demonstrated that people can read the emotions of others by just looking at their touch.

Heslin has identified five haptic areas:

Functional/professional which expresses task-orientation

Donald Walton, in his book, stated that touching is the ultimate expressions or confidence between two persons. But this isn't often seen in formal or business relationships. Touching emphasises the unique message that is being conveyed by the initiator. Walton wrote that "if a word of praise comes with a touch to the shoulder, that is the gold star in the ribbon."

Social/polite that demonstrates ritual interaction

Jones and Yarbrough conducted a study that found touch communication to be the most intimate and involving method of communicating with people. This helps them maintain close relationships. Jones and Yarbrough outlined that strategic touch can be described as a series of touching, usually with an ulterior purpose or hidden motive. They are using touch to make someone do something.

Friendship/warmth to express an unusual relationship

Love that expresses an emotional attachment

Public touch can act as a tie sign that shows other people that your partner "taken". The 'tie signs' that show others that a couple are together include holding hands, clasping hands, and wrapping their arms around one other. Burgoon Buller and Woodall found that the use of 'tie marks' is more common in courtship and dating than it is between married couples.

Proxemics

Proxemics (or spatial relationships) is another noteworthy area of body language nonverbal. Edward T. Hall first introduced proxemics back in 1966. It's the study of measurable distances that people experience when they interact. Julius Fast explained in Body Language that the signals we send or receive through body language to others are reactions to their invasions of our personal territory. Proxemics forms an important part Body Language.

Hall also created four distinct zones in the which most men work:

Friendships and interactions between family members are possible through personal distance

Close phase – 1.5-2.5 feet (46-76cm)

Far phase: 2.5 to 4ft (76 to 122 cm)

Social distance allows for interaction among acquaintances

Close phase – 4-7 feet (1.2-2.21 m).

Far phase – 7-12 feet (2.1-3.7 m).

Public Speaking with public distance

Close phase – 12-25 feet (3.7-7.5 m)

Far phase: 25 feet (7.6m), more

Other than physical distance, the degree of intimacy between con-senants can be determined by the "sociopetal-fugal-axis", also known as the "angle formed at the axis the conversant's shoulders".

It is important for you to know that the range of proximity between two people varies depending on their culture. Hall suggested that "physical touch between two persons... can be perfectly right in one cultural, and completely taboo the next".

Latin America may have people who may seem completely strangers, but they can often be in close contact. They often greet each others by kissing on their cheeks. North Americans prefer shaking hands. Although they have made some contact with each other through the shaking, there is still a certain amount between them.

Tone

"The body also influences our breathing patterns, which can have a profound effect on the quality of the words we say."

Particular voice tones are related with specific types of bodylanguage. If someone's voice is happy and their body language conveys this impression, it will be reflected in their body language. This is due to the change in a person's mood and their breathing pattern. This can influence their body language and intra abdominal pressure (IAP), and this has an impact on their tone. When someone feels confident, their IAP (breathing pattern) will improve, and their voice tone will sound more powerful and fuller. When they feel anxious or irritable, their IAP, breathing, and voice will become shallower. Because a person's mood can be seen in their breathing patterns - which is a key influencing factor for both tone of vocal and body language - their voice will tend to reflect the same feelings as their body language. Notably, digital voice-based devices such as Amazon.com Alexa tend to reduce or eliminate the sound IAP. The voice lacks a human-like fullness and sound more robotic.

Tone can be affected by how your body positions are. When someone speaks while hunched back in a seat, it may obstruct their breathing system. If they were to sit straight up, the breathing system would be free from obstruction and their tone of voice would be clearer, more energetic, focused.

Attitude

"Human communication has many parts. It is difficult to judge the feelings expressed.

Your body language plays a significant role in how you communicate your attitude to others. Albert Mehrabian asserts that 7 % of communication during a conversation about feelings or attitudes (i.e... like/dislike), 38% are via words and 38% via tone of speech, while 55% of communication is done via body language. This is also known by the '7%-38%-55% Principle', and it is often studied in studies of human communications. Although there is much debate regarding the proportion that each of these factors should be given, it is generally accepted that bodylanguage plays a major role in determining how a person feels.

People may alter their body language or attitude to influence how they relate to others. You can influence the way another person responds by changing your body language. For example, an interviewer who is formal may convey a more business-like attitude. This might encourage the interviewee or other interviewees, for instance, to give more serious answers. This can help them develop a better working relationship. An informal attitude conveys more of a casual, open-minded impression. This could be used as a way to get more honest answers from interviewees, to foster a deeper relationship, and to make them more forthcoming.

Readiness

With your team mates, you can form impressions about each other's strength and unity, as well their mood and body language. Physicality is obviously stronger in sport but you can also read the mood by looking at your teammates, sitting together, on a basketball court.

It is possible to convey the impression that you are ready to act through your body language. This can be seen in both the physical and mental senses. These states can influence the person's tone and body language, as well as their overall body. The state of being more ready can also be described as being at high levels of energy and intensity. Contrary to unreadiness states, states of readiness usually involve deeper breathing patterns, increased excitation of nervous system, and increased heart rate. These physiological effects can have a significant impact on the appearance of skin, including how full and supple it is. When a person is in a state to be ready, their skin will appear fuller and tauter, while it will look thinner and more flaccid. This can be translated as a greater intensity and prominence of the visual effects when you are prepared for physical exertion.

Are you ready for physical exertion?

This is how someone prepares for exertion. They prepare their body by warming it up and mentally focusing in on the task ahead. They are now ready to take on the world. To an observer they look 'pumped up. Their body language is a sign that they are ready to move quickly and with more energy.

Aggressive behavior mimics or exaggerates a person's appearance of physical violence to intimidate them. Because the torso appears larger than usual, this is known as a 'bracing/ballooning'. This preloading of the body's muscular system for action is sometimes called a loading up'. Aggressive posturing might also involve clenching of fists.

You are open to social interaction

It is also possible to feel more open to social interaction by pumping up, although this effect is less intense. The different intentions may mean that a person must prepare for social interaction by preparing their neck, shoulders, and throat to speak, as well their arms and legs to gesturing and their head for speaking. Before giving a speech, it is necessary to prepare for how to stand. The body language of a person who plans to interact socially will change if they prepare to talk. This is a sign that they are more confident in their ability to communicate with others and will be more open to them. For example, someone may be sitting with their arms out in front of someone with open body communication. If they were seated with closed-body language they might be facing the other person with their arms folded. This could signal their disinterest or discomfort in the conversation. Each body language signifies a willingness for the conversation to move in a particular direction. This might indicate that the person is ready to get up. You may also want to end the conversation.

To help you prepare for a social interaction, you can use body language to warm up. This may include power poses such as standing tall, raising your arms toward the sky, or looking like Superman with your hands on your hips.

Universal vs. specific to a culture

Scholars have been debating for decades whether facial expressions, including body language, can be understood universally. Darwin's (1872), evolutionary theory suggested that facial expressions of emotion were inherited. However, scientists have been hesitant to ask if one's culture is a factor in bodily expressions. There are two main models to the theories.

Model of cultural equivalence

The cultural equivalence concept predicts that individuals must be equally accurate in understanding and interpreting the emotions of both ingroup members and outgroup members. (Soto & Levenson. 2009). This model stems from Darwin's evolutionary theory. Darwin noticed that humans and animals exhibit similar postural expressions such as anger/aggressions and joy. These similarities support the evolution argument that social animals (including humans) have a natural ability to relay emotional signals with one another, a notion shared by several academics (Chevalier-Skolnikoff, 1974; Linnankoski, Laakso, Aulanko, & Leinonen, 1994). Darwin observes similarity between animals and people, while the Cultural Equivalence Model identifies similarities in human expression across cultures.

The strongest piece of evidence supporting this model was a study carried out by Paul Ekman & Friesen (1971), which showed that preliterate members from Papua New Guinea recognized the facial expressions displayed by individuals from the United States. Culturally isolated, the Papuan tribesmen were not exposed to US media and there was no way of cross-cultural transmission.

Cultural advantage model

The cultural advantage model on the other side predicts that people from the same race "process visual characteristics more accurately" and "more efficiently than people of different races". Familiarity with nonverbal accents can also help improve interpretive accuracy.

There are many studies that support the cultural advantage model and the cultural equivalence theory. However, there is general agreement that seven emotions can be universally understood, regardless of cultural background.

Recent studies have revealed that pride and shame expressions are universal. Tracy and Robins (2008) concluded the expressions of pride include a more upright posture and a nonDuchenne smile. An expression of shame involves covering or turning down the face.

Applications

Basicly, bodylanguage is an involuntary and unconscious phenomenon which contributes to the process for communication. It has been proven to be useful to harness body language both in action, and also for comprehension, however. With large volumes of guides and books published that help people to become aware of bodylanguage and how it can be used to benefit them in certain situations, the use of bodylanguage has seen an increase in commercial application.

Body language is used in many areas. Body language can be used for instructional purposes in areas such second-language acquisition or to enhance teaching subjects like mathematics. As a substitute to verbal languages for those who cannot hear or speak, body language can be used in a similar way. The use of body language in the detection and prevention of deceit has been done in both law enforcement and poker. Sometimes, Language Barrier might be an issue for foreigners. In order to communicate effectively, it would be a good idea to use body language.

Chapter 11: Popular Hand Gestures and their Meanings in Different Cultures

While gestures can be helpful for some, they may be offensive in others. Knowing their meanings will help you avoid offending others. Learn more about the meanings of popular gestures and how they change from one country to the next.

First, you will see the "V," sign on your hand. This hand gesture was first used during World War II as a sign for victory. It is a sign that the word begins with the letter VI. In Eastern culture, especially Japan, Koreas, Thailand, and China this signifies that a person appears cute while being photographed. The negative meaning of the "V" sign in countries like Australia and New Zealand, Africa, Ireland, New Zealand, Australia and New Zealand is however. The sign could be considered offensive to others and can land you in trouble.

It is not appropriate to use the word "OK" for everyone. Scuba divers can use a hand gesture to indicate their approval, where the tip is touched by the thumb. This is called "A-okay". This sign is widespread in many cultures. In Latin America and Europe it is considered offensive.

Crossing fingers can be interpreted as a wish for luck. It can be used to predict good things. It is an indication that a person wants to be saved from evil.

Facebook's "like" feature is illustrated by thumbs up. This is a commendation for Western culture. This is an insult to the Middle East, Russia, Greece and West Africa.

In some Western countries, females may use the index finger curl to seduce males. Use this gesture in Far East countries with caution. It is, for example, a sign to call a dog in Japan. This is considered to be a sign of someone's death in Singapore.

Some people have different beliefs. It is important to avoid offending anyone when you are visiting someone else's country. For harmonious relationships to continue, it is essential to understand hand gestures and how they differ from one culture's.

Chapter 12: Body Language Of A Flirting Woman

Here's what's good! This is what your heart has been expecting. Everybody and their cousin is looking to find love. You've wondered if the person you are in love with feels the same. But asking them isn't the right thing. But what if they don't feel that way about you.

You would look like an absolute creeper! (Gasp!) Okay, let's just get to the point and learn how to interpret body language. This will help you not look like the love obsessed, creepy person you are. Just kidding! A little humor can make a big difference, especially when you are dealing with heart issues. When ladies feel drawn into you, they will be a lot more unobtrusive. Some ladies will coyly pass on signs that she is interested, but it's possible for some to be coy. Here are signs that you might be interested by a lady's body language.

1). Pay attention at her feet. Although it sounds strange, attitude is determined by how her feet look. If her feet are pointed in your direction, it means she is showing you that she is attracted. But not if she points her feet away from your face.

2). She touches you. You may feel her touch your hand when she is talking to you, bumps into you, or taps on you. This is a subtle way to tell if she's into you.

3). She's nervous. Attracted women can also exhibit signs of nervousness, such as when they chew their gum super fast, play with their watches, or mess around with their jewelry. It is possible for her to play with her watches, chew her gum super fast, fiddle with her phone and even take her jewelry apart. These are signs she may be shy or nervous. She might be trying to reveal parts of her bodies that emit pheromones by doing these things during conversations with you. If she is attracted by you, your opinion of her is very important. She could feel a different way about you, which could affect her self-esteem. When she does this, it's because she wants to expose parts of herself that emit pheromones.

4). Keep your eyes on her legs. Women who are interested will usually cross their legs to show interest in you. Her top leg will also be pointed in your direction, similar to her feet. When this happens, you will know that you've attracted her attention. If she touches her legs with her fingertips, or uses her hands to stroke them, it's likely that she is trying draw your attention.

5). Being a copycat. It is not that she is trying be annoying if she mimics your movements. She is just flirting with me! She is probably unaware of this synchronized behavior as it feels so natural. Nonverbally, she is saying that her understanding of you and your feelings is the same.

Now, what if she's not so into you? Here are some signs you need to pay attention to:

The eyes don't lie. If a woman avoids eye contact with a man, especially if he is looking at him, that's usually a sign she isn't interested. If a woman shows interest, she will hold eye contact with the you and, if necessary, pick up the contact again. If she looks at you while you talk to her, and your eyes do not focus on hers, this means she has become disinterested in the conversation.

The use of closed-body language. Closed body language can be used by someone who is interested. Closed body communication may include crossing her arms, putting their purse between you guys or sitting in a stoop. These actions are a sign of disinterest. She may also be trying to shut you out, or putting a purse between your hands.

Avoid mouthing. You can see the contents of her mouth. If she behaves distastefully when you are having a conversation with him, then pay attention to what she says.

There are many strategies a lady can use when she wants to have a closer look at a man she likes. The lady who raises her eyebrows while simultaneously raising her eyelids is showing delight. Different expressions can include but not be limited to fast flickering while keeping eyecontact, holding eyecontact and grinning or smiling. If a young lady seems timid, she may look at you and smile or stare at you.

Men, being the detail-oriented people we sometimes are, can often miss clear signals that a girl is interested in their company. Monika Moore says men often miss the first signs of a woman being interested in them. Women must look up three times to catch a man's attention before they notice. Keep in mind that actions speak louder then words, so pay close attention and be aware of what signs she is giving. The woman you are seeing now could end up being the woman you marry later.

Chapter 13: Common Patterns In Interpreting Behavior: Hands And Arms

We express so much of our emotions through our hands and our arms. A soft, intimate hug of just a little can signify love. An angry slap is an indication of anger. How accurate our arms and hands are in completing tasks determines a lot about our productivity. As an adjunct to verbal expression, movements of the arms or hands are obvious. Let's now look at some subliminal signs we can receive by analysing our hands and arms.

Our arms can expand and we appear larger than usual. This could be used to explain how big an object, person or object is. It might also be a subtle indicator of dominance or aggression. It also signals spatial awareness. A person could extend their arms to signal they are aware of space. This can be thought of as "marking their territory." It is sometimes compared to hugging. This embrace is a sign of safety or protection. This is how many mothers are seen welcoming their children.

Because we use our arms and fingers to gesture, they are extremely descriptive tools that help us express our emotions. If the arms are raised it is often a sign that you are frustrated or overwhelmed. As protection, you can imagine an overworked person clutching their hands to their ears.

A sign that someone is feeling good or bad may be the crossing of their arms. As stated above, crossing your arms means that you are feeling anxious, shy, afraid, or confused. After a child does something inappropriate, the frustrated parent will likely cross his or her arms towards him/her. It is not a good sign that the arms are crossed. This happens when a male is taunted. They may actually be holding their arms back as a form of protection from their anger. These hidden fists could be an indication that someone is holding back from doing something they regret.

People who are vulnerable to violence or exposed to it may feel a strong dislike for those who speak with them. Even a simple gesture could signal a fight response. This is usually a scare tactic that aims to emphasize the importance of the arms moving forward. We fight with our arms as well as our hands so the connection between these two is alarming.

Hidden intent refers to the position of the arms behind the backs and away from the eyes of the person you are engaging with. A person might lack confidence or try to hide their fear by wiggling their hands behind them. This isn't a sign of a lying person. This may be because the person feels uncomfortable or is avoiding saying something.

When facing out, the elbows might be a silent cries for space. The individual may want others to stop pursuing them. The actions of young children will show this easily. Even toddlers who cannot communicate verbally may extend their elbows with a sharp motion to point space. As adults, we subconsciously do the same thing as toddlers to protect ourselves.

The hands communicate very clearly using their gestures. One gesture can be used to call for participation. A second movement could cause conflict. It is a sign of peace when your hands are crossed, with the thumbs under. This sign of peace is common in East Indian gurus. It's a symbol of their peaceful, giving natures and thanksgiving. They desire to shine this light on others through their body movements. This is often a symbol of dignity. When the hands are placed over the belly button, the fingers touch and the palms open, it's called a logo for dignity. This person wants to prove their partner that they are competent, professional, and conscientious.

Hands are key indicators for direction. To point towards specific areas of interest, our fingers serve as a guide. It is possible to show submission by placing your hands gently on your knees with your palms up, especially when looking at the other person. This is how women engage, while flirtatiously trying to express their interest. Hand gestures can also be used to signify movement. A palm facing an individual can signal disapproval and dismissal. The person is trying to physically keep the other person out of their sight with their hands.

It could signify boredom, brainstorming, and even deciding when the hands touch the faces. It is an indication that someone is trying get out of an unfavorable situation by holding their palms to the face and lifting the cheeks. It is clear that the individual is disinterested even when it's not obvious. But, the index might indicate deep thought. The firmness of the grasp and the positioning of fingers can also be a telling sign.

High stress situations lead to excessive shaking. Nervousness can cause hands to shake uncontrollably. This is also a sign of intense hunger. This indicates a lack of food and causes the fingers and hands to become unsteady. You may also feel a slight shake when you are being confronted or caught lying. They may get so angry, the shakes will be their way of expressing it.

To describe the size and stature, we use our fingers. Similar to arms, they are used to show movement, emphasize gravity, and describe the weightiness or the importance of a topic. They're the main way that we gesture, and they can add excitement to a conversation or story. If a person is confident when working alongside their arms, their hands can often indicate how confident they are. Touching creates heat and community, which can help people to connect. If carefully studied, movements of the hands or arms can give clues to a person's disposition.

Chapter 14: How to Spot A LIE - Key behavior that indicates deception

If you can detect deceit, it will allow you to make wise decisions about your associates. When someone lies, it causes the body to go into a state of shock. The trained eye is able to see the small differences that may occur. The body does not lie, even though words might seem to reflect the truth. You can be deceitful by hiding what you feel. Control is often performed in a poor manner, which can lead to dominant cues that signify deceit. Dishonesty has many consequences. People lie as a subconscious protection mechanism. They are either trying to hide their negative behavior, or they are protecting their reputations. Even though they might not embellish a story much, they are trying to keep their life boring. They need to find others who enjoy them. There are many lies that can be told.

One company breaks down deceit to four categories of explanations, and uses them:

Anxiety - they try to mask the fact that their nervousness is real

Control- gestures of control or smiles that are forced on the body or a grand plan for stopping it from moving

Distraction: The person is trying to distract you with their lies by frequently pausing or performing bodily acts in between the answers. They believe they're making your stories credible by performing such grand gestures.

Persuasion - Deceit may result from the desire to convince someone to perform an action that is in the liar's favor.

Joseph Tecce, a Boston College researcher revealed six reasons why individuals still live, in addition to their unique character traits.

1. Protective Lies are used to preserve the reputation of the perpetrator or protect the victim from undue danger. They want to maintain their social status by hiding true behavior.

2. Heroic Lies: These people will strive to make the world a better place. Sex and the City's popular episode featured Carrie and Stanford at the mixer. Stanford was curious to learn more about a handsome gentleman in the space. Carrie was asked by him to travel with him and determine whether he was gay or straight. She approached him and informed him of Stanford's interests. In total repulsion, the man viewed Stanford from across space. Carrie then told her hopeful friend that the handsome man she was talking to was straight. She wanted to protect her friend's self-esteem by not telling the truth.

3. Playful Liars. This is where the liars are playful and exaggerate their stories, in an attempt to entertain listeners.

4. Ego Liars. Ego lies will cover up their mistakes to protect their reputations, or their status.

5. Gainful Liars - These are people who lie for personal gain.

6. Malicious Lies: These are those who use psychological challenges to try and take revenge or harm others.

Many people are so clever at lying that they need to master the art. Sociopaths and psychopaths are both deranged, and they have no emotional connection to the lies. Because they're so attached to the lies, it's difficult to identify their inaccuracies. They even believe the lies. Although they may believe the lies, there might be other causes. Let's look at the signs and characteristics of deceitful people.

A lie starts when the head moves quickly. A liar may quickly move his head after being asked a question. Many of the most convincing signs of deceit are found in the face. Timing is the key to expressing our emotions. Researchers have discovered that people hold their expressions for between one and four seconds. A person who lies or fakes an emotion will usually hold the expression for a longer period of time. A person's symmetrical alignment can also help to detect insincerity. If you want to know if someone is honest, look at how evenly the emotions are spread across their faces. A liar might express their emotions dominantly on one side. Our speech and body movements should complement each others. So, if someone tells you how beautiful they feel while frowning and crossing his arms, you can safely conclude that they're not genuine.

Nervosity can be correlated with excessive body movement. The body naturally engages in tiny movements even without the presence or hysteria. However, Professor Leanne Brinke of the Haas School of Business says that individuals who are as still and composed as statues need to be examined. "You should be even more cautious of those who are still as still as a statue," she says. This might be due to the human instinct to fight or flee. They're shocked to find out that their behavior has been caught. They have lost all control at that point and feel exposed. To feel some control, they tighten their abdominal muscles.

It is also important to notice where they hold their hands when being confronted. Do they cover what is in front of them? Throats? Chests? They're providing a subtle distraction that helps them escape the reality. They are not trying to conceal the reality. Verbal cues are another indicator of deception. An indication of nervousness is excessive repetition, stuttering, or clearing the throat. They are desperately trying for time to reply.

The eyes have always been closely associated with deceit. We discussed previously the connection between interest and dilation. When we see something we like or are interested, our eyes dilate. In a relationship, the pupil dilation is a sign of a loss in interest. You can ask your partner if you think your outfit is amazing. But, their pupils will reveal the truth. The presence of excessive darting in the eyes or avoiding eye contact is a sign that there is some deceit. Another possibility is that the person may be trying out to show aggression but refusing to look at others' eyes. Are they really as tough and strong as they seem? The right brain controls auditory processing as well big picture ideas and deciding. Individuals who look downward and to the right are trying to find something. They'll gaze to the right when they dream of living there. Notice how they keep repeating the same motion when lying. It is interesting to note that they are trying not to recall a past memory but rather seeing something that doesn't exist.

Deceit can also be seen in the body. You will notice an increase in the speed of the person's breathing. Their chest could move faster and their breathing sounds louder. Their elbows, shoulders, and elbows are stiffly raised. This motion is often depicted as being caught in cartoons. The robber might inadvertently stop and raise their shoulders. They are trying their best to be defensive and protect themselves. Psychics use exposed palms to reveal truth. Although controversial, many readers examine the open palms to find hidden emotions, predict future outcomes, and decode personality. The palms of truth can suddenly close when someone lies. It's their subconscious way of not being eager to speak the truth.

Even though it is important to be able detect lies, simply being able is not enough. Effective communication can be combined with understanding to help uncover lies, and find solutions.

Chapter 15: Charisma

Some people have the gift of being able to simply walk into any room and turn heads. They have charisma and a magnetic presence that grabs everyone's attention. These people have the potential to be the alphas, leaders or top dogs.

One thing is for sure, we're not born charismatic so we must all be able to learn it.

Charismatic people radiate confidence. This is one of their most distinctive attributes. It is important to keep that popularity going by their body language. Your body language is key to being liked and making friends. Your openness should inspire friendship, not weakness. We all have weaknesses. But we can learn to hide them. That smile that you display must appear genuine and not fake.

Charismatic people are always good listeners. It's all in the attitude. You must have a pleasant disposition and give substance and value to what you say and do. Encourage others and motivate them to take action. Remember that nonverbal emotions are reflected in verbal movements. At the very least, it is worth trying to look the part.

However, not everyone can feel that warmth towards people. But, it is possible to become more relaxed by being around others. Focus on other people, and you can let your thoughts drift away from your own emotions. You can bring your mind into sync with the movements of your body. This will show in your attitude, and your movement if you have used relaxation techniques.

It's a lot like the natural smile that releases stress hormones. It will make you feel taller.

What impression do you get of someone who is sitting in a slouching chair? They won't have any impact on your perception so they will likely be overlooked. Some people may think they are tired or drunk, so you don't pay much attention to them.

Try to treat each person as if they are your closest friend. This is how to make friends.

Friendships, and Acquaintances

It is not easy to make someone feel at home. This skill will help you build new friendships. You cannot achieve this by using words only. Your reactions are what will make it possible.

They are subconsciously scanning your body language. Now is the best time to make that first impression count. Although we know that we shouldn't judge based on so little information, the reality is that it happens. It's not something we think about, and it isn't something we are conscious of. To improve your communication skills, make it your new goal to use gestures more conscious. You can greet strangers with a smile. Give it a real smile so it shows through your eyes.

Oculesics: Eye Contact

Engage them with eye to eye communication. We have a 10-second average time that we look at one another, so make sure to take advantage of it. Keep your eyes open, even when the other is looking away. It's important for you to let your confidence shine through. However, be cautious and not overdo it. This could be seen as an obstacle, which would not get you off to a good start at your first meeting.

Pay attention to their reactions when you introduce yourselves. They may not be making eye contact or smiling, which could indicate a lack in confidence. It is your responsibility to make sure they feel safe and more confident in their company.

Haptics -- The Power Of Touch

Take their entire hand and hold it tightly if you are required to shake hands. Don't pretend that they have any disease or that you don't want to touch their skin for too long. Wait until they release you and then let them lead. Don't force it, as it could be seen aggressive. Not grabbing their arm from their sockets will get them the positive reaction they desire.

If they seem nervous, or lack in confidence, then try a handshake. Gently place your other arm on top of theirs.

Haptics, a form of touch-communication, is also known. This is often reserved only for those you love or trust. Your actions are showing that you are willing to go against the grain and do what is necessary. If it makes them feel more relaxed, this is a great way to show them that you are not afraid to do the unexpected. If done right, you will appear warm and open-minded.

Listen And Mirror

It is important to pay attention to your nonverbal movements in order for you to be able understand others' movements. Listen to the words of others and carefully observe their movements. Only then can your reactions be correct, even to the point of mirroring. If they smile, you should return the smile with a warm open smile.

Even if someone else folds your body, resist the urge. Do your best to be the leader and display an honesty that reflects you. If they start to mimic you, you may be able to help them relax.

Space Proxemics

Concentrate on how far apart your position is from the person that you are speaking to. Do not invade their private space. However, you can be close enough to make them feel heard.

Be aware of what you are saying and how it feels. This is difficult because it goes against the grain. You can put aside your emotions for a brief time. Believe that you like the person who you are talking to. Even if they don't know you or are not familiar with your situation, this is a good idea. By doing this, your body language will be open and relaxed. It is possible that it will lead to a friendship lasting a lifetime or a significant working acquaintance.

Chapter 16: Tools To Say No

This chapter presents a range of tools to help the reader face different manipulations. These are helpful weapons, and they will be of great use to anyone who has understood the mechanisms and overcame any fears or mental blocks that might have prevented them opposing manipulation.

No matter the type or degree of manipulation that you may encounter, there are some principles that you must follow.

The Tools Of Analysis

It is essential to first understand the situation. It is important to ask yourself a few questions. What is it? What is the problem?

A well-framed situation can be characterized when one can answer the questions clearly and use a precise formulation. He wants... He would like to...

This helps to avoid getting lost, or falling for problems that do no exist or are not relevant to you. Many people find it difficult to think clearly and avoid making useless statements by trying too hard to answer questions that they don't want or appropriating other people's problems.

You can find a situation that you have been able to help someone who has not asked you for anything, and you will be surprised at how the outcome.

Identify the Types of Manipulation

This work is crucial to avoid being manipulated or getting out. In reality, when we ask ourselves if we're being manipulated by a charmer (or one who guilts or is respectable, or an authoritarian), we can take a step back, gain insurance, and let ourselves be less susceptible.

After realizing that it is a charming manipulator we become more alert because we know it is difficult for us to refuse his request. This awareness keeps us from falling into his trap or prepares for how to get out. Once we identify a manipulator who is guilty, we will compare the information he provided with what he requested. We will also be less upset with his attacks, and we will be better equipped to defend ourselves.

When we expose a well-meaning manipulator, we can see and listen from a different perspective. If we are willing to give up the blasphemy then we can see clearly through a child's eye and help him understand his intentions.

Finally, when we recognize that we are being controlled by an authoritarian manipulator, our vulnerability to his schemes decreases. We are well aware of his attempts for us to please him by playing on our old desire of love, on our instincts of obedience and on guilt we may feel when refusing to obey.

You can reduce your risk of being a victim by identifying the manipulator. It's never too early to make this identification. But, the faster you act, the more likely we will be caught.

Point Them

If you feel manipulated or want to clarify any misunderstandings, it is important that you check regularly whether one understood the nature the request. It's enough to tell the manipulator exactly what you feel, and then ask him to clarify.

You feel invited by a friend, even though he does not explain if it is to repair his vehicle. You can let him know. "If I understand, you want my help to complete the campaign. He will need to answer the question clearly in one way or another. You will then have your answer concerning the manipulation.

You can now take stock and see what is confusing. Now, your refusal can be expressed with legitimacy without any trace of guilt.

A type II manipulator will try to sell an insurance policy to you. For example, he might say, "If I understand correctly, please suggest that I purchase this insurance policy which protects me from such & such, while my existing contract covers me." He is embarrassed to respond, "Yes, however, with my ..." Without allowing him to continue, you could say to him, "Well, thank you. I understand you well, and there is no other thing to add." We will be leaving, but we thank you.

This development again gives us the confidence to put an end of manipulation and end the conversation with no guilt.

After a long conversation that allowed Mathilde and a charming manipulator to get to the bottom of her concerns (who was also very powerful) she can confidently declare, "If I understand correctly, you want to mar me so I come and stay at home to look after your cat when it is not there and to also do the housework and cook the meals." Does that really sound like what I'm looking for in life?

Most manipulations are founded on poorly stated demands. When you confirm with the manipulator you understand what he wants you to, you can no longer be controlled by him.

Tools of The Refusal

It can be difficult to express oneself or voice disagreements. Some prefer to avoid problems. Even if they devalue them, each new difficulty is for them an additional proof of inability to solve it.

Others attack those who are being tricked. They are aggressive and hostile, and their features become hardened. They can also wear an ironic smile or express disapproval. This is a way to demonstrate that we don't let ourselves be fooled. This attitude, however, shows one is not secure and fragile.

Aggressive behavior can reveal latent fear, a desire to revenge or a degree frustration. Anything is possible for a skilled manipulator to exploit.

You don't have to flee or attack. There's an effective way to assert your rights and defend them without inciting hostility. This is called serene affirmation.

The Serene Assertion

This last one is about being authentic. One must not hide emotions. Assert yourself serenely. Playing your cards on a table is one thing. The other is to be comfortable and to find a balance while controlling the environment. This technique can be used to fight type II manipulators because it is believed the manipulators are open for logical discussion and understanding.

A Technique Comprising Several Stages

The preparatory Phase: To begin with, we must think. We need to be able to discover and understand both the motivations and the hidden benefits that he is seeking from manipulating others. You can also do it very quickly and easily.

The second stage corresponds to the meeting between the manipulator and the user:

Give details and objective descriptions of the situations you are living in and how he treats you. Don't accuse him or express guilt.

Discuss with him any emotional or material effects (stress, fatigue ...) resulting from his manipulation) and the upheavals caused by this. You can share your emotions, concerns, and critics with him. This is about talking to yourself and what's happening, not about the other person.

Offer a solution or realistic modification to the situation.

If he doesn't know what to do, show him.

You could create conflict by telling a smoking smoker to "Go outside and enjoy your smoke", as his primary purpose isn't to stop smoking but to have fun while he smokes. Therefore, it is likely that he feels attacked by our request. This would be unfair for him.

The other side of the coin is that it will be easier to communicate to him, "I get that you want me to smoke, but it makes me sick." Would you be able smoke outside the area where you work?

This second method considers the needs of those who have been frustrated. It allows them to change their attitude and makes it easier for them to see the things he's been trying to do.

It is possible to say to someone, "Stop doing these, you annoy us." Or you could say, "Stop doing these things. It annoys me." We accuse him and make his life miserable.

This message often makes it feel like someone is being shamed, humiliated. Criticised, rejected or blamed. To say to someone tapping his pen on a table, "Stop irritating me," is a sign of disrespect and often leads towards retaliation.

One could, on the other hand, say to him, "When you make a small noise while tapping your pen on the desk, it keeps me from concentrating." Please stop and allow me to finish my job. This conveys your respect for the forms of serene affirmation.

From here, it is very likely that the interference stops immediately.

It would have never happened if it had been said in an angry voice, "Stop teasing"! Messages like this are not usually the most effective in reaching the goals that were hoped for.

When a message has been properly written, it is perceived as a call of help by its recipient. It informed him that his problems were understood. This, in turn, encouraged him and invited him to pay attention to our concerns. The message dispels emotion and sets the stage for positive change. The message is a rebuttal to make it a wish. This reflects nonverbal feelings.

It is important to respond quickly and efficiently

It is also important to quickly respond to type II manipulators.

Why wait?

A manipulator is more powerful if we don't say no. It gives him an impression of weakness by not responding. He can also interpret our silences as hesitation. He can gain even more assurance by using new arguments to convince or confuse us. The manipulator will play with us by making it difficult for us to respond.

How can you be sure to answer correctly?

This question is very interesting as it involves knowing how to measure our answer's effectiveness. You can risk exacerbating an authoritarian manipulator and being crushed by him if your response is too aggressive. On the other hand, if your answer is too weak, it will make you appear less credible and won't consider our opposition. So how do we find the right measures?

As is often the situation, the answer will come from the person who actually created the problem. A manipulative attack can be resisted by using a power that is 90% greater than the manipulator.

If someone shouts at you, do not shout louder because it will not help. Although it can be helpful to talk calmly at times, this is not possible with a manipulator who will benefit from showing that he has more power. You can answer him in the exact same tone, with a strong and firm voice, though slightly lower than yours, and he will pay more attention. He will look at you and say, "Here is somebody who does not allow himself to be outdone." It would be safer for me not to be suspicious.

Your quick and confident responses will demonstrate that you are strong and not afraid to confront him. In simple terms, the manipulator will view you as dangerous. If you agree, he will try to negotiate something.

Not being able to respond quickly and efficiently does not mean that you should be unable to think on your feet. You can learn from your own experiences. Stay in the limbo and write short sentences. You do not need to defend your opinion. Do not be rude or aggressive. Be friendly and humorous. But, above all, don't get involved in the manipulator's game.

One must be able and able to give a strong response. But, without exaggerating.

This technique is not available on demand. It takes time to respond well and quickly. It all depends on how the circumstances are. It is more that a tool.

Acceptance with Restrictions

It doesn't matter if you are asked for something. There are always things you can accept and things that you can refuse.

A friend requests me to lend some money to him. His banker has been calling him every single day, and he has run out. I am willing to say yes, but instead of saying no: "I understand that your banker calls you every day and asks you to lend me money. But I can only give you three months. After that, you will have to pay your taxes. I will be in the exact same situation you are if I do not receive my payment on time. That's what you can expect from me. Now it is up to YOU to make that happen.

The Rules Of The Limited Remembrance

As you have read it, reformulate the request to the manipulator. "If I understand your request correctly, ..." This should not be considered a judgment. This should be used to verify that you are talking about the exact same thing. This helps to avoid innuendo and unspoken remarks.

You can express partial refusal beginning with the positive. Your restrictions will then legitimize it. The condition that ..." I agree with the manipulator. A partial refusal is closer towards an outright acceptance than it is to a refusal.

Ask the manipulator for his opinion. "What do you think?" This is all I can do. You decide! ..." You are the one who can make that decision.

The purpose of the limited rejection is not defeating the manipulator. As much as possible, it is about ensuring that everyone benefits while the other person feels not wronged. This is known to be a win/win scenario.

The Ten Commandments

These steps are vital. They are often sufficient to end minor manipulations. It is possible, however, that the manipulator will respond to your request.

If you say no to a charming manipulator, he can try to make it seem like you are guilty. If you can hold on and reply to his retort by denying, you will eventually win. One example: You might say, "You can see the things like this but I see them otherwise!" This is a declaration of your right and freedom to think and reason independently of what others think.

The more one is certain about oneself, it is easier to challenge and freely express what one believes. This will encourage the manipulator not to ignore us but to respect and fear us. This indifference will eventually discourage the manipulator if he continues to hold that attitude.

These rights are important to understand and keep in mind to help facilitate this legitimacy.

The Ten Commandments to Be Indifferent to Manipulation

I have the right NOT to be perfect.

I have the option to be logical.

I have the right to choose not to know.

I have the freedom to not deceive.

I have the rights to my own opinion.

I have every right to be unpopular.

I have the freedom to sometimes be indifferent toward certain problems.

I have the option to change or withdraw my opinion.

I have every right to not be justifiable.

I have the rights to think of myself.

You can add rights to the list you cannot grant or wish to claim. Post this list and these Ten Commandments somewhere you can find them easily every day.

In this way, you will become increasingly indifferent to manipulators' arguments.

Inventing New Weapons

To be able to overcome manipulation one must imagine how another person would behave. Whatever the individual, the key is finding and using another perspective that will allow both of us to transcend our reflexes for submission and find other solutions.

Take a look at a situation of manipulative authoritarianism and ask yourself: How would you defend yourself against it? What would you say? What would he think?

The answer could be someone (his superior, his spouse, or any other such person that would resist him), or an authority concept such a lawyer. A leader, a policeman or nurse. Or anyone who, according to you, could completely dominate the manipulator. It does not matter what you are imagining, but imagine the words and actions of this real or imaginary person to master the manipulator. This information is invaluable because it reveals hidden talents or resources.

Conclusion

Communication is key to our world. Communication between humans has been necessary since infancy. Communication is constantly evolving due to technology advancements and times. But body language as well as non-verbal skills remain an essential part. These skills can add flavor and life to your communication experience.

Even in business, although it is often a formal affair. However, body communication remains a fundamental part of any business. Along with nonverbal skills, improving on this and other communication skills makes business communication an entirely new experience. Since business transactions require at most two parties, communication becomes a tool that must be sharpened for the precise execution of business targets and ideas. As part of human development, companies should organize pieces of training and seminars on communication and communication-related topics such as body language, non-verbal skills, and emotional intelligence.

These areas are important for both inside and outside of the business world. The long-term benefit of this type of training is that it will help businesses and organizations.

These skills are very helpful in times of extreme stress and confusion.

Sometimes, a few mistakes or inactions can make it impossible to complete a long-awaited business deal. Sometimes, all you have to do is smile and make your client happy when you present your proposal or in a meeting. You cannot overstate the importance of body language in business.

Otherwise, you're just as good as anyone in Wonderland.

Many times and on multiple platforms, business outfits meet with customers when they launch or during advertisements, promotions, or on a tour. This is when grammar is crucial because you need to convince people or large groups of people that your business is worth their time. Being able understand body language, and other non-verbal skills is vital because these skills allow you solve difficult problems and help others. If there are unfortunate circumstances such as litigation or dispute, it is possible to save millions of dollars and accept genuine remorse.

This part of communication is vital in a world such as ours, where we communicate even if we do not realize it. Effective communication involves the recipient receiving the intended message the way that the sender intended and decoding it. The body language and the non-verbal skills of communication are essential for a business to stay in business.

www.ingramcontent.com/pod-product-compliance
Lightning Source LLC
Chambersburg PA
CBHW050401120526
44590CB00015B/1773